The Death Of Alexander The Great

A Reconstruction Of Cleitarchus

by

Andrew Michael Chugg

2009

First Edition

© 2009 by Andrew Michael Chugg. All rights reserved.
ISBN 978-0-9556790-2-5

In memoriam Hephaistion Amyntoros

The Death of Alexander the Great
Contents

1.	Introduction	1
2.	The Reconstruction of Book 13 of Cleitarchus	5

Is Curtius mainly translating Cleitarchus; Poetical Devices in Cleitarchus; Fragments that Fit the Thirteenth Book; Babylon as the Metropolis; Re-Ordering Curtius on the Mutiny at Opis; The Palace Regiment of the Hypaspists and the Somatophylakes; The Large Lacuna in Curtius; Hephaistion's Pyre; Hephaistion the Demigod; The Cause of the Death of Alexander; How Did the Leading Men Split after Alexander's Death; Arrhidaeus the Fool; The First Division of the Satrapies; Last Plans; Antipater & Cassander as Regicides; The Itinerant Corpse

3.	Book 13: July 324BC – July 323BC & Beyond	50

The Flight of Harpalus; The Exiles Decree; The Mutiny at Opis; Death of Hephaistion; The Cossaeans; Death in Babylon; Aftermath & Entombment

4.	Organisation And Sources	84
5.	Bibliography	88
6.	Acknowledgements	94
7.	Index	95

1. Introduction

This monograph presents the latest stage of an ongoing project to reconstruct the most influential of all the ancient accounts of the career of Alexander the Great: the history of his reign compiled by Cleitarchus of Alexandria, which has been lost since antiquity. I began this reconstruction with the three Indian books of Cleitarchus, which have been published together as *Alexander the Great in India*. The work presented in the present volume constitutes a reconstruction of all the Cleitarchan material between the end of *Alexander the Great in India* and the conclusion of Cleitarchus' history of Alexander. The highlights of the events recounted in this volume are therefore: the flight of Harpalus upon Alexander's return from India; Alexander's proclamation of the Exiles Decree and the reactions of the Greek states; the mutiny of Alexander's Macedonian troops concerning the discharge of the veterans and how it was quelled; the death of Hephaistion; Alexander's winter campaign against the Cossaean bandits; the funeral of Hephaistion; the death of Alexander in Babylon; the political turmoil in the aftermath; the rites accorded to the king's corpse and its ultimate entombment. It is an inference from my research that these matters were all treated successively in the thirteenth and final book of Cleitarchus.

It is my intention eventually to produce as complete a reconstruction of Cleitarchus as may prove feasible and so supporting material already published in *Alexander the Great in India* has the scope of the entire work. However, the next section of this volume particularly provides a more detailed analysis of issues pertaining to the reconstruction of *Book Thirteen*.

The reconstructed text is not merely a simple translation of passages from the surviving secondary sources, although virtually every sentence is founded upon evidence from those texts. Instead it has been necessary to meld overlapping and intersecting accounts together and continually to assess which source should have pre-eminence in the case of (usually slight) disparities. Furthermore, I have thought it fitting to attempt to echo the evidently flowery literary style of Cleitarchus to some extent, especially in the case of speeches and descriptive passages. To this end I have occasionally resorted to poetical devices including rhythmic or metrical passages, incidental rhyming or mere assonance and especially alliteration. Yet it would also be true to say that some of this embroidery is already echoed in the surviving Latin and Greek texts of Curtius, Diodorus and even Justin and Plutarch. In this sense my own text is not merely a reconstruction, but also an evocation of the original.

Different passages may be attributed to Cleitarchus with widely varying degrees of confidence. Therefore, I have indicated the approximate confidence level using a textual hierarchy running from lowest to highest (the latter being defined as attributed fragments of Cleitarchus from surviving ancient texts). This is implemented as follows: *italic;* plain text; ***italicized bold;*** **simple bold;**

The Death of Alexander the Great by Andrew Chugg

<u>underlined simple bold.</u> Although grey text has been reserved for connecting passages, where the Cleitarchan version is unfathomable, it has not been necessary to resort to its use for *Book Thirteen*. Subject to a few minor exceptions, it is possible to read the reconstruction at a variety of confidence levels by ignoring all text below the desired level of fidelity.

This reconstruction is particularly founded on the premise that Curtius and Diodorus (Book 17 & Book 18.1-4) are largely abridgements of the History of Alexander by Cleitarchus, whereas Justin (Books 11 to 13.4) and Plutarch's Life of Alexander are believed to contain substantial Cleitarchan elements (this has been argued in detail in *Alexander the Great in India* – the interrelationship between various of the lost and extant ancient sources is summarized in Figure 1.1). Although I cannot be absolutely sure that Curtius did not employ another major source, the process of performing the reconstruction to date has had the incidental consequence of accumulating many minor points of evidence such as pose a cumulatively strong case that Curtius is in fact substantially (though not entirely) a Latin translation of an abridged version of Cleitarchus' Greek text. In particular, it has thus far transpired that this hypothesis resolves most difficulties without generating significant inconsistencies.

However, reconstructed text entirely based on material from either Curtius or Diodorus 18.1-4 or Justin 12-13.4 is indicated at a relatively lower level of confidence. Higher confidence is assigned to material exclusively derived from Diodorus 17. Still higher confidence is vested in cases where there are detailed matches between these sources and the highest confidence rests with the attributed fragments of Cleitarchus, although they are sadly sparse.

If the premise of a common source for the surviving texts were correct, then it would be expected that a relatively smooth and cogent version of the prototype could be reconstructed by merging them. However, if any of the extant sources had employed a significant secondary source, then it would be anticipated that the attempt to define a prototype that explained all the material in each of them should encounter numerous contradictions. It is a conclusion of the present research that it has been possible to reconstruct all three of Alexander's years in India and the final year of his reign plus its aftermath without encountering significant contradictions when integrating all the appertaining material in Curtius and Diodorus (with the obvious exception of a few passages in Curtius where that author is clearly offering his own comments and one instance, where he attacks Cleitarchus by name with reference to Ptolemy's version in a matter that concerned Ptolemy.) This is an important result, because it tends to reinforce the premise that Curtius and Diodorus at least are essentially abridgements of Cleitarchus. Such an inference is not at all obvious in reading those sources individually.

In the case of Justin, we know from his manuscripts that he epitomised Trogus, although the latter probably used Cleitarchus (or else Timagenes who in turn used Cleitarchus). More difficulties tend to arise in reconciling his words with

Introduction

the tradition from the other Vulgate texts, as might reasonably be expected for such indirect transmission. A straightforward example is that Justin attributes the advocacy of Heracles' claim to the succession to Meleager, whereas Curtius suggests (much more credibly) that Nearchus presented his case. Yet in fact this is easily explained as either an accidental consequence of successive stages of epitomisation via Trogus or else just another of the gross errors which are plainly attributable to Justin's rather careless epitomisation of Trogus. The process of reconstruction has also indicated significant amounts of Cleitarchan material in Plutarch, by virtue of some striking parallels between my text (reconstructed from Curtius and Diodorus) and some of Plutarch's anecdotes. But it is equally obvious that Plutarch used many early sources (as too did Cleitarchus), so I have used his material sparingly and at low confidence.

Neither do I intend that this should be the final and immutable version of the reconstruction, but rather hope that it may evolve and be revised in the light of new evidence or arguments as they emerge.

Finally, I would also commend the account of Cleitarchus to those readers who have little interest in the technical niceties of source research for Alexander studies. Cleitarchus' account rested on its literary merits for centuries in winning its place as the most popular version of Alexander's campaigns among the Hellenistic Greeks and the Romans. I believe that it retains good measures of readability, atmosphere, coherence and accuracy even in the present metamorphosed and imperfect form, sufficient anyway that it may be read in isolation as an authentic breath of the distant past by readers who are relatively unfamiliar with the particulars of the history of Alexander the Great.

The Death of Alexander the Great by Andrew Chugg

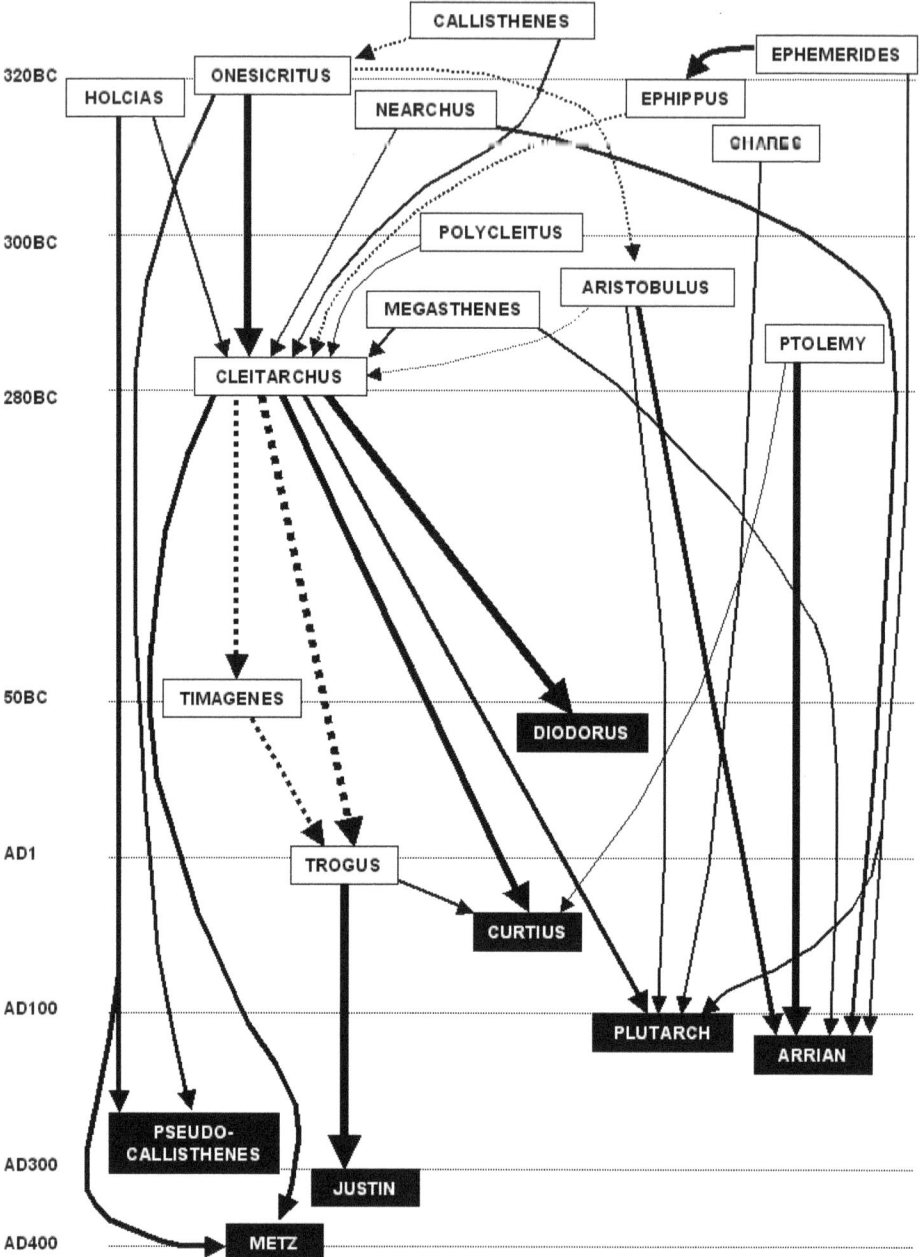

Figure 1.1. Relationships between ancient authors on Alexander's campaigns especially pertaining to Cleitarchus (white in black box = extant; and vice versa).

2. The Reconstruction Of Book 13 Of Cleitarchus

Is Curtius mainly translating Cleitarchus?

Orthodox wisdom holds that Curtius is an original author, who fashioned a unique history of Alexander's reign in gloriously rhetorical Latin in the early Imperial period, most probably under the first Claudius. The case for this view is superficially strong. In particular, there are several passages where it is indisputable that we hear the authentic voice of Curtius himself. Key examples would be Curtius' comment on the inaccuracy of Cleitarchus in reporting the presence of Ptolemy at the Mallian siege and Curtius' remarks at 10.9.3-6 drawing a parallel between the elevation of Arrhidaeus and the succession of his own emperor to the purple of Rome.

Furthermore, whereas many passages in Curtius have strong and direct echoes in Diodorus, whence we infer that they shared a common source in Cleitarchus, there are also a number of instances where the account of Diodorus appears wildly disparate from Curtius' version. Since Diodorus is known generally to have followed single sources closely over long sections of his "Library of History", it would seem to follow that Curtius must have interspersed his gleanings from Cleitarchus with material from other sources.

This reasoning made perfect sense to me at the outset of the reconstruction project, at which stage my opinions on the matter were relatively orthodox. However, having had cause to examine the source texts far more attentively in the course of the reconstruction, my original confidence in the conventional wisdom has been substantially undermined. It is apposite to try to explain why.

Firstly, I have become keenly aware that modern editors or translators have inferred a number of instances of the use of the first person singular by Curtius, which actually lack any manuscript authority. Examples in the context of my reconstruction of the Death of Alexander include: *comperimus* at Curtius 10.10.5, which is unambiguously first person plural, but is translated as "I have ascertained…" by John Yardley in the Penguin edition; then again at Curtius 10.10.12 Vogel changed the manuscript reading from *refert* to *refero*, and he has been followed by other modern editors, thus giving "I report what is recorded rather than believed" whereas "Here is related what is recorded rather than reckoned reliable" would be more faithful to the source material.

Evidently, orthodox views on the nature of Curtius' work are intruding so far as to insinuate subtle re-writes into the source text to make it fit the hypothesis of its being an original work more conspicuously. I do not even suggest that this tendency has been conscious, for in fact it generally seems to have been inadvertent; or at least the question of the originality of Cleitarchus has not been to the fore in the minds of the perpetrators. The reason that this should nevertheless disquiet us is the background context of the quasi-political mission of Tarn and others in the 20th century to disparage and marginalize Cleitarchus as a source on Alexander. Downplaying Cleitarchus' influence upon Curtius harmonises tunefully with Tarn's litigious approach.

There remain, of course, some valid instances where Curtius genuinely interjects comments, but it could be posited that these are generally of the nature of footnotes in a modern translation. Some may have been inspired by early scholia (ancient marginal notes) that became appended to the traditional text of Curtius. For example, it is interesting that the observation that Ptolemy effectively contradicted Cleitarchus on the issue of his presence at the Mallian siege is also explicitly pointed out by Arrian, *Anabasis* 6.11.8. Conversely, Diodorus and the Metz Epitome avoid mentioning Ptolemy's presence, even though it must have been in the text of Cleitarchus that they were following. An obvious way in which several authors could have been led to highlight or suppress this error would be for a scholium to have appeared in some early manuscript of Cleitarchus that happened to become the prototype for many subsequent manuscripts of his work disseminated within the Roman Empire. Curtius additionally realised that that Timagenes had made the same error, but he could have known this through his evident familiarity with the work of Trogus.

More hints that the very sentiments of Cleitarchus pervade the words attributed to Curtius may be inferred from the pronounced vein of cynicism in his text. This is often manifested in ways that are hugely incongruous, in the light of the biographical evidence on Curtius. It is not feasible to review all the issues here,[1] but it is likely that he was the same Curtius who was the Roman Proconsul of Africa under Claudius. Yet this wealthy and influential servant of the Claudian dynasty speaks of pearls as the "vomit of the retching surf" (8.9.19) in railing against their supposed corrupting influence on society, which he also seems to regard as recent, despite trade between Europe and India having flourished for nearly four centuries in Curtius' era. Even more out of place is his vigorous condemnation of the luxurious lifestyle of the Indian kings, where most of his complaints refer to behaviour that would seem quite modest relative to the outrageous antics of his own imperial masters. Modern authorities on Curtius have seen all this as evidence for a covert streak of asceticism in this pillar of the imperial state, but, when we do hear Curtius' own voice clearly at 10.9.3-6, it is ringing in its support for the emperor and clearly intended to be publicly disseminated. It is a much more straightforward explanation for the overtly cynical sentiments in Curtius that they were understood by his audience to be mere Latin translations of the Greek words of the philosopher and rhetorician

---

[1] For discussions of the dating and identity of Curtius see Atkinson's Commentaries on Curtius and Waldemar Heckel's Introduction to the Penguin translation of Curtius.

The Reconstruction Of Book 13 Of Cleitarchus

Cleitarchus, who is actually known to have associated with the Cynics (e.g. Stilpo) and even used them among his own sources (e.g. Onesicritus).

If indeed Curtius was the Quintus Curtius Rufus who was Proconsul of Roman Africa at the time of his death in AD53, then there are potentially yet more absurd incongruities, which I can only resolve by supposing him to have operated as Cleitarchus' translator. In particular, it is instructive to examine in detail a problem with some ancient rhinos in Curtius 8.9.16-17. The manuscript readings (with a few alternatives indicated) seem to have been:

Aves ad imitandum humanae vocis sonum dociles sunt. Animalia invisitata/inusitata ceteris gentibus nisi invecta. Eadem terra et rynocerontas/rinocerotas/rinocerontas alit non generat. Elephantorum/elefantorum maior est vis quam quos in Africa/Affrica domitant et viribus magnitudo respondet/respondit.

The statement regarding the elephants is also in Strabo 15.1.43. He attributes it to Onesicritus (Alexander's helmsman on the Indus river voyage), who was also undoubtedly a major source for Cleitarchus. By the 17th century Freinshem was giving the passage as:

Aves ad imitandum humanae vocis sonum dociles sunt. Animalia inusitata ceteris gentibus, nisi invecta. Eadem terra et rhinocerotas alit, non generat. Elephantorum maior est vis, quam quos in Africa domitant; et viribus magnitudo respondet.

The same form persisted through to C. H. Weise in 1840, but by 1841 Julius Muetzell had dropped the *et* in front of the rhinos. E. Hedicke (Teubner 1908) saw that it is fairly preposterous for the text to suggest that the rhinos were not native to India. In fact the Great One-Horned Rhino is native to the foothills south of the Himalayas and was certainly encountered by Alexander's expedition. It is at least unlikely that an eyewitness source like Onesicritus would have suggested that it had been imported. Furthermore, the preceding sentence has alluded to Indian animals that were unknown (or at least uncommon) elsewhere, so one would naturally expect the rhinos to have been mentioned as a specific example. Hedicke therefore proposed a rather heavy-handed emendation:

Aves ad imitandum humanae vocis sonum dociles sunt. Animalia invisitata ceteris gentibus nisi invecta. Eadem terra rhinocerotas aliis ignotos generat. Elephantorum maior est vis quam, quos in Africa domitant, et viribus magnitudo respondet.

Which was translated by John Rolfe (Loeb 1946) as:

"There are birds which can be taught to imitate the sound of the human voice. The animals are unknown to other nations, except such as are imported from that country. The same land produces rhinoceroses, which are unknown to other peoples. The strength of its elephants is greater than those which men tame in Africa, and their size corresponds to their strength."

Other 20th century editors took a different approach. Bardon in 1947 seems to have sought to lessen the difficulty by arbitrarily dropping the entire sentence beginning *Animalia*, even though it exists on perfectly good manuscript authority:

Aves ad imitandum humanae vocis sonum dociles sunt. Eadem terra rhinocerotas alit, non generat. Elephantorum maior est vis, quam quos in Africa domitant; et viribus magnitudo respondet.

Yardley followed Bardon's text in the 1984 Penguin translation:

"Birds can be trained to imitate the human voice and the country also supports a population of rhinoceroses, though this is not indigenous. Its elephants possess greater strength than those trained in Africa and their size matches that strength."

The logic here seems to be that Curtius believed African rhinos to have been imported to the Himalayan foothills from Africa in the 4th century BC, which is a little preposterous. But Curtius probably did know about African rhinos: a rhino was exhibited at Pompey's games[2] in 55BC and Martial[3] mentioned the African rhinoceros, which also appears on a quadrans of Domitian. Why then would he have written, as Hedicke would suggest, that they were unknown outside India? I think the likely answer would be that he considered that he was translating his Greek source (Cleitarchus) rather than compiling a fresh account.[4]

Although I feel Hedicke had the right idea regarding what this corrupted passage is trying to say, his particular emendation is rather too gross to be easily credible. I suspect instead that the *et* in front of the rhinos that was dropped so long ago, might be a mistake for *est* (i.e. copulative use of the verb *esse*, as also occurs for the elephants in the ensuing sentence), in which case we would not be very far from: "The same land possesses rhinoceroses, elsewhere not indigenous."

How, then, would I explain gross disparities between Curtius and Diodorus? I cannot address every instance here, but let us take the passages on the accession of Abdalonymus as an example case. Curtius gives what seems a correct version of the story with Abdalonymus appointed King of Sidon before the siege of Tyre on the recommendation of Hephaistion, whereas Diodorus does not mention Sidon, but has Abdalonymus instead appointed to rule Tyre *after* its fall. Prandi, Bosworth and others have highlighted and discussed the case of

---

[2] Pliny, *NH* 8.71, whose description, despite a solitary horn, appears to be following Agatharchides, *De Mari Erythraeo* 72, who described a rhino from Eritrea or Northern Somalia.

[3] Martial, *Liber de Spectaculis* 9.2 & 22.1; other early mentions of rhinos in Rome include Suetonius, *Augustus* 43.4 and Dio Cassius 51.22.5 & 55.33.4.

[4] According to Athenaeus 5.201C a rhino from "Ethiopia" was displayed in the Grand Parade of Ptolemy Philadelphus in Alexandria in 275-274BC; however, Cleitarchus probably wrote at an earlier date and was himself probably closely following the primary account of Onesicritus.

The Reconstruction Of Book 13 Of Cleitarchus

Abdalonymus,[5] because it appears to present an intractable local difficulty for the reconstruction of the Cleitarchan version. It has been believed that Cleitarchus mistakenly made Abdalonymus king of Tyre and Diodorus followed him, whilst Curtius and Trogus used a more correct source in placing events at Sidon. However, Curtius 4.1.26 mentions that an area surrounding Sidon was added to Abdalonymus' dominions by Alexander. Perhaps Cleitarchus threfore mentioned that he was given control of Tyre after its fall and that was what prompted Diodorus to tell the story of his original appointment as a king in the context of the fall of Tyre. Perhaps Diodorus in his original manuscript correctly referred the story of Abdalonymus' appointment back to Sidon in Section 17.47, having noted his appointment as king of Tyre in Section 17.46.6. If so, given the curious order in which Diodorus presents the matter, an ancient editor of Diodorus would obviously have assumed that the mentions of Sidon were an error for Tyre and incorrectly corrected them in some later manuscript that became the prototype for our surviving versions of Diodorus. This seems to constitute a logical and viable way of explaining the confusion through an understandable rather than a crass error, which also allows that Diodorus, Curtius and Trogus were all still following Cleitarchus. Although it might be objected that Philotas was made garrison commander in Tyre according to Curtius 4.5.9, I cannot see that this excludes Abdalonymus as its king. I would submit that this scenario makes more sense of the matter than the conventional suppositions and serves as an illustration of my point that holding fast to the view that Curtius is almost entirely Cleitarchus yields credible reconciliations of textual problems.

The question might be posed of why exact parallels between the texts of Diodorus and Curtius are not more numerous, if they are both essentially epitomes of Cleitarchus? In response I would point out that the virtually exact parallels are in fact quite numerous (they are listed in Table 2.1 for the convenience of the reader). However, I would go on to note that Diodorus rarely precisely translates Cleitarchus, but continually paraphrases and contracts him. Indeed this case has been made for me by Bosworth, who notably and correctly points out that where the Fragments of Cleitarchus are echoed in the text of Diodorus, we can see evidence that Diodorus perpetrated some serious mangling: Bosworth particularly employs the example of the 440 talents that Alexander gleaned from the fall of Thebes.[6] My final comments on this issue are

---

[5] Luisa Prandi, "Fortuna è Realtà dell'Opera di Clitarco" in *Historia Einzelschriften* 104, Steiner, Stuttgart, 1996, p.102; A.B. Bosworth, "In Search of Cleitarchus: Review-Discussion of Luisa Prandi: Fortuna è Realtà dell'Opera di Clitarco" in Histos (University of Durham, electronic journal of historiography), Vol. 1, Aug. 1997, pages 6-7 of 9.

[6] He also informatively flourishes the actual mangling in a case where Diodorus is known to have used extant passages of Polybius as his source: A.B. Bosworth, "In Search of Cleitarchus: Review-Discussion of Luisa Prandi: Fortuna è Realtà dell'Opera di Clitarco" in Histos (University of Durham, electronic journal of historiography), Vol. 1, Aug. 1997, pages 4-5 of 9.

that the work of Curtius was on a grander scale than that of Diodorus and they had quite different objectives for their texts: Curtius delighted in the rhetoric and cynicism of Cleitarchus' style, whereas Diodorus sought to extract a sharply pared down *precis* of the bare facts of the history of Alexander's conquests.

Several scholars of Curtius' work have been at great pains to demonstrate that he resounds with reverberant echoes of his predecessors Trogus and Livy.[7] Their case seems well made, but it cannot greatly detract from the hypothesis that he is translating Cleitarchus for the simple reason that both Trogus and Livy were themselves demonstrably influenced by Cleitarchus. Hence it would be difficult to contradict the view in the case of any significant match between Curtius and either of them that both Latin writers were simply imitating Cleitarchus. To those who have said that Curtius borrows and retouches Roman history from Livy, I propose that Livy borrowed and retouched Greek history from Cleitarchus.[8] If so, then the readiness with which Livy's plagiarism can be recognized through the text of Curtius becomes a testament of the fidelity with which Curtius reproduced Cleitarchus.

It is beyond the scope of this sub-section to treat this issue comprehensively, since there are many lines of evidence that must be scrutinised in detail. Instead, the ambition of this introductory tract is to challenge the casual assumption that the orthodox view of the nature of Curtius may be regarded as secure. It is always ground for suspicion when ostensibly sound foundations are found to be built on sand like the insolvent islands of Arabia.

Poetical Devices in Cleitarchus

Pearson has noted that there is some evidence that at least part of Cleitarchus work may have been written in a type of blank verse known as Asianic Rhythms.[9] He cites several passages in Diodorus 17, where tiny tweaks reveal snatches of lyric verse, and adds a couple more instances in Fragments 19 and 22 of Cleitarchus. In addition, it is known that the so-called Asianic style was briefly popular around the beginning of the 3rd century BC and was extensively employed by other contemporaneous historians of Alexander: notably by Hegesias of Magnesia. The use of metrical devices by Cleitarchus also provides a possible explanation for the existence of numerous poetical turns of phrase and much highly rhetorical material in Curtius and Diodorus 17.

It has been impractical to attempt to reproduce any consistent metre in the reconstruction of Cleitarchus in English: my view is that it would have interfered too much with the accurate translation of the meanings in the source

---

[7] E.g. W. Heckel in Section C of his Introduction to the Penguin translation of Curtius (1983).

[8] R. B. Steele, "Quintus Curtius Rufus", *AJP* 36 (1915), p.409.

[9] Lionel Pearson, *The Lost Histories of Alexander the Great*, American Philological Association, 1960, p. 213.

The Reconstruction Of Book 13 Of Cleitarchus

material. However, I have insinuated certain rhetorical and poetical devices in a less systematic and more fitful fashion insofar as may be accommodated within a faithful reproduction of the source texts. In particular, I have injected a fair amount of alliteration and more occasional snatches of metre and couplets of verse. Hopefully, this may give an impression of the lyrical pretensions of the original without overburdening the reader with pretentious poesy.

Fragments that Fit the Thirteenth Book

The longest Fragment to survive from Cleitarchus' final book is actually a passage cited from the work of Theopompus by Athenaeus concerning Harpalus' mistresses (Jacoby F30 of Cleitarchus = Athenaeus 12.50 or 586CD). However, Athenaeus concludes his quotation by noting that Cleitarchus had given the same account. Theopompus joined the court of Ptolemy in Egypt after Alexander's death, whereas Cleitarchus was a resident of Alexandria under Ptolemy. Hence it is likely that Cleitarchus was familiar with Theopompus' writings and borrowed from his material on Harpalus. Certainly, there is a close connection between the quotation from Theopompus in Athenaeus and the abridged Cleitarchan material on Harpalus' mistresses at Diodorus 17.108.5-6.

Theopompus seems to have been broadly hostile towards Harpalus. He was a pupil of Isocrates of Athens, a friend and supporter of Alexander's father. Theopompus also benefited from Alexander's patronage, which permitted him to return from exile to his home island of Chios. Hence he was inherently politically aligned with Alexander in the context of Harpalus' flight and the Exiles Decree, but this need not detract from his criticisms, which may well have been justified.

The only other Fragment from Book 13 of Cleitarchus that is considered reliable is the mere mention that Cleitarchus wrote about an Embassy sent by the Romans to Alexander in Babylon (Jacoby F31 = Pliny, *NH* 3.57). Arrian 7.15.5 also mentions a couple of obscure writers (Aristus and Asclepiades) who had recorded that the Romans had sent representatives to Alexander, although Arrian omitted mention of Cleitarchus in this context. The ancient sources are generally in agreement that other envoys from central Italy (e.g. Etruscans) were among the throng in Babylon, so it need not be controversial that Romans were also present. What is more curious is the impression that Cleitarchus particularly drew attention to the Romans among so many disparate delegations. This is because the Romans were not well known in the Greek world until Pyrrhus' campaigns in Italy from 280BC. The implication is either that Cleitarchus' list of envoys was very lengthy and comprehensive or that he finalised his text after 280BC and highlighted the Romans because they had recently figured prominently in Pyrrhus' dispatches from Italy. Badian has also suggested that Pliny's comment that Cleitarchus' account was "more than mere rumour" may mean that Cleitarchus actually witnessed the Roman audience with Alexander, but this is surely to read too much into an ambiguous phrase.[10]

There are also two Fragments attributed to Cleitarchus by name that Jacoby has nevertheless considered doubtful, but which fit quite neatly in specific contexts within the reconstructed text of Book 13.

1) A short passage on not mourning friends excessively (Jacoby F41 = Maximi, *Eclogae* 6.761A[11]) is very much the sort of comment that Cleitarchus might have made concerning Alexander's elaborate arrangements for the funeral of Hephaistion, hence I have fitted it to Section 13.33 of the reconstruction.

2) A comment on kingly behaviour not being inculcated by royal trappings, specifically the diadem (Jacoby F52 = Antonii, *Melissa* 2.1, p.1005C) provides an extraordinarily apt addendum to the episode where the prisoner sat in the throne and donned the diadem, which is covered in Section 13.40 of the reconstruction.[12]

Having also managed to fit a couple of the "doubtful" Fragments of Cleitarchus to Books 10-12 in *Alexander the Great in India*, it is beginning to seem highly likely that all the moralizing comments attributed to Cleitarchus by Antonius (a Greek monk of the 11th century AD) in his Melissa and by Maximus Confessor in his *Eclogae* (Anthology) are indeed abstracted from the *History Concerning Alexander* by our author, despite Jacoby's expression of dubiety.

Babylon as the Metropolis

Curtius 10.2.12 makes the interesting assertion that Alexander's Macedonian troops believed at the time of the Opis Mutiny that the king planned to establish the permanent seat of his government in Asia (incorporated in the reconstruction of Cleitarchus in Section 13.8). In fact there are several strands of evidence that point to Alexander having regarded Babylon as the chief city of his Empire. Tangible evidence survives in the form of many of the tetradrachms of Alexander, which were minted at Babylon and which bear a mu-tau-rho monogram, designating it as the *metropolis* or mother-city (Figure 2.1). Furthermore, Strabo explicitly attests to the significance of Babylon in Alexander's eyes:

Strabo 15.3.9-10: "Alexander carried off with him all the wealth in Persis to Susa, which was also full of treasures and equipment; and neither did he regard

---

[10] E. Badian, "The Date of Clitarchus", Proceedings African Classical Associations 8 (1965), p.10.

[11] A.k.a Maximus Confessor, *Loci Communes*.

[12] Some (e.g. Michael Wood, *Footsteps of Alexander*, 1997, p.225) have linked the prisoner on the throne incident to the ritual of having a scapegoat king to divert the bad luck in times of ill-omen, although this is supposition, since our sources instead report the matter as an unfavourable sign from heaven.

The Reconstruction Of Book 13 Of Cleitarchus

Susa as the royal residence, but rather Babylon, which he intend to build up still further; and there too treasures lay stored… At all events, Alexander preferred Babylon, since he saw that it far surpassed the other [cities], not only in its size, but also in all other respects."

Above all, perhaps, Alexander's decision both to hold Hephaistion's funeral in Babylon and also to build his friend's permanent memorial in the ashes of the pyre is an important indication that he viewed the metropolis as his de facto capital.

Figure 2.1. Posthumous tetradrachm of Alexander minted in Babylon – the city is designated as the Metropolis ("Mother City" = Capital) by the Mu-Tau-Rho monogram in a wreath at the left edge of the reverse (Author's Collection).

Re-Ordering Curtius on the Mutiny at Opis

There is a peculiarity in the manuscript tradition of Curtius regarding the placement of the fragmentary chapter 10.4. The surviving paragraph of the Latin text appears to be a reproach to Alexander by one of the thirteen condemned mutineers swiftly followed by their collective execution by drowning in the river (Tigris). This is incongruous and anachronistic, because we have already read at Curtius 10.3.4 that news that the executions of the mutineers had been carried out had reached the troops. Obviously, it looks as though the material in Curtius 10.4 has been misplaced and should actually be positioned somewhere between the arrest of the thirteen mutineers at 10.2.30 and news of their execution a few sentences later at 10.3.4. As John C. Rolfe has noted in the Loeb edition of Curtius, an important early 17th century editor of Curtius, Johann Freinshem, inferred a lacuna between 10.3.2 and 10.3.3, which precisely suits the insertion of the material in 10.4.

It is understandable that modern editors of Curtius have not felt at liberty significantly to re-order the manuscript tradition in this respect, although I am surprised that most modern editions do not even draw the reader's attention to the anomaly. Nevertheless, since my purpose is the reconstruction of Curtius' source, Cleitarchus, I have felt obligated to make the obvious correction in the present work. Thus I have inserted the material of Curtius 10.4 into Cleitarchus 13.13, whereas material from Curtius 10.3.3 onwards follows it in Cleitarchus 13.14.

The Palace Regiment of the *Hypaspists* and the *Somatophylakes*

Diodorus 17.110.1 mentions that Persian recruits a thousand strong were appointed to a palace regiment of the *hypaspists* (literally "shield bearers") in the wake of the mutiny of the Macedonian troops [at Opis] evidently scheduled to perform duties at his court. This must be derived from Cleitarchus and is incorporated in Section 13.17 of my reconstruction, where it is merged with a matching account from Justin 12.12.4. It appears that this unit derived its royal association from its provision of *doryphoroi* (literally spear-carriers) who performed traditional palace guard duties for the king of the type where one man stood either side of an entrance, so that they could cross-spears to bar entry to interlopers. The implication of the Persian appointments is that the original Macedonian members of the regiment had sided with the mutinous troops and were to be replaced by loyal Persians.

It would be reasonable to infer that this is the same body of troops that Arrian regularly refers to as the *Royal Agema of the Hypaspists* (e.g. Arrian, *Anabasis* 1.1.11, 1.8.4, 2.8.3, 3.11.9, 3.13.6, 5.13.4…).[13] In addition to the shared name and royal duties, both regiments seem to have had a nominal strength of a thousand men. And yet an extraordinary modern orthodoxy would have it that Diodorus elsewhere refers to these palace *hypaspists* as *somatophylakes* (literally "bodyguards"). This engenders considerable confusion due to this latter term also being used to refer to the seven elite personal bodyguards of the king, who were his highest-ranking courtiers. Yet, if *somatophylakes* was his normal term for the guards regiment, why should Diodorus (and Cleitarchus?) have anomalously referred to them as *hypaspists* with palace duties in the context of the mutiny?

The orthodox interpretation particularly derives its ambivalence concept for the term *somatophylax* from a range of four instances in Arrian where it has been supposed that it refers to a unit within the overall brigade of *hypaspists*. Let us review these instances, which are interpreted by Heckel[14] (and others) to show that Arrian uses *somatophylakes* to mean the unit that he elsewhere refers to as

---

[13] It has been argued (e.g. Heckel, *Marshals*, p.245-6) that Arrian uses the Greek term *agema* as a name for a particular regiment of guards. But in fact *agema* seems to have been phonetically equated to the Latin military term *agmen* for a regiment or an arrayed block of troops (there is a similar pairing between *ile* [Greek] and *ala* [Latin] for a wing of cavalry). Other instances (Diodorus 19.27-29, Plutarch, *Eumenes* 7) indeed suggest that *agema* merely means a regiment and only refers to a particular regiment when given a qualifier such as "Royal" (e.g. Polybius 5.65.2).

[14] E.g. W. Heckel, *The Marshals of Alexander's Empire*, Routledge, 1992, s.v. The Somatophylakes.

The Reconstruction Of Book 13 Of Cleitarchus

the *Royal Agema of the Hypaspists*. Is it really impossible or even merely unlikely that these *somatophylakes* are instead references to the seven elite Bodyguards?

a) Arrian, *Anabasis* 1.6.5: "As Alexander saw only a few of the enemy still occupying a ridge, along which lay his route, he ordered his *somatophylakes* and *hetairoi* to take their shields, mount their horses, and ride to the hill; and when they reached it, if those who had occupied the position awaited them, he said that half of them were to leap from their horses, and to fight as foot-soldiers, being mingled with the cavalry. But when the enemy saw Alexander's advance, they quitted the hill and retreated to the mountains in both directions. Then Alexander, with his *hetairoi*, seized the hill, and sent for the Agrianians and archers, who numbered 2,000. He also ordered the *hypaspists* to cross the river, and after them the regiments of Macedonian infantry, with instructions that, as soon as they had succeeded in crossing, they should draw out in rank towards the left, so that the phalanx of men crossing might appear compact at once."

b) Arrian, *Anabasis* 3.17.2: "[Alexander] then took the royal *somatophylakes*, the *hypaspist* infantry, and 8,000 men from the rest of his army, and, under the guidance of the Susians, marched by night along a different road from the frequented one. Advancing by a route rough and difficult, on the same day he fell upon the villages of the Uxians, where he captured much booty and killed many of the people while still in their beds; but others escaped into the mountains."

c) Arrian, *Anabasis* 4.3.2: "But when [Alexander] observed that the course of the river, which flows through the city when it is swollen by the winter rains, was at that time nearly dry and did not reach up to the wall, and would thus afford his soldiers a passage by which to penetrate into the city, he took the *somatophylakes*, the *hypaspists*, the archers, and Agrianians, and made his way secretly into the city along the channel, at first with a few men, while the barbarians had turned their attention towards the military engines and those who were assailing them in that direction."

d) Arrian, *Anabasis* 4.30.3: "[Alexander] remained quiet until they began their retreat; then taking 700 of the *somatophylakes* and *hypaspist* infantry, he was the first to scale the rock at the part of it abandoned by the enemy; and the Macedonians ascended after him, one in one place another in another, drawing each other up. These men at the concerted signal turned themselves upon the retreating barbarians, and killed many of them in their flight."

It may be conceded that these *somatophylakes* seem to be mentioned in the same task forces as very large units and that it is strange that seven men should matter among forces of hundreds or thousands. But is this enough to conclude that a larger body is meant? It needs also to be recalled that Arrian's source is probably Ptolemy, who was himself a member of the seven elite Bodyguards. Homeric principles of celebrating the heroism of warfare, which Ptolemy is likely to have espoused, would allow that special attention should be paid to the exploits of key warriors and commanders. Hence some good reasons to suspect that these references actually refer to the Seven may be posited:

1) The first reference 1.6.5 makes it clear that its *somatophylakes* were mounted. Whereas it is not impossible that Alexander had given horses to some of his *hypaspist* infantry, it does stretch the meaning of the term infantry in what was evidently a battle situation. In fact the only other unit involved in this particular action is the *hetairoi* (literally "companions"), which could mean the fifty or so Friends of the king in this context. Furthermore, the enemy upon the ridge are "few", so it is not necessary to envisage vast numbers in this action.

2) In extracts b) to d) the *somatophylakes* are mentioned in combination with the *hypaspists*, but as though they were a separate unit, which is slightly strange if they were in fact a regiment from within the *hypaspist* corps.

3) In passage d) the very curious number of 700 men are included in the task force. This does not correspond to the probable strength of 1000 for an *hypaspist* regiment. In fact chiliarchs (commanders of 1000 men) and pentakosiarchs (commanders of 500 men) are mentioned as attending on Alexander at his deathbed (Plutarch, *Alexander* 76.3 and Arrian, *Anabasis* 7.25.6). This comes from the *Ephemerides*. Hence we have evidence for units of 500 and 1000 men in Alexander's army, but never 700 men. Therefore the specific figure of 700 begs explanation and the desired rationalisation is to hand, since we know that there were precisely seven elite *somatophylakes*. What if Ptolemy had actually written that Alexander took the *somatophylakes* with seven centuries of the *hypaspists* on this mission? We have both an explanation for the total and an explanation of just why the *somatophylakes* were mentioned, for they commanded the individual hundreds for the purpose of the mission.

4) If point 3) were correct and reflected standard practice, then it could explain the combination of mentions of the *hypaspists* and the *somatophylakes* in extracts b) & c) too.

In summary, I cannot accept that it is at all necessary to believe that a different unit than the Seven is meant in these four standard references.

Several instance of the use of *somatophylax* in the text of Diodorus have been deemed to reinforce the orthodox concept of ambivalent terminology.

1) Firstly, the incoming recruits to the *paides basilikoi* (literally "King's Youths" a.k.a. "Royal Pages") in Asia at Diodorus 17.65 are stated in C. Bradford Welles' translation to be "sent by their fathers to serve as

bodyguards [*somatophylakes*]". This has led to the supposition that Royal Pages could also be referred to as a third species of *somatophylax*. However, the Greek text actually reads *pros ten somatophylakian*, for which a more literal translation would be "sent by their fathers *with a view to becoming bodyguards*". This is far more ambiguous. It ccould mean that they would soon have the responsibility of personally guarding the king (which was within the scope of their duties). But it could also easily mean that their fathers hoped that they would ultimately graduate from the Pages to become members of the Seven – a very sensible explanation of the motivation of the fathers, which Diodorus has probably grossly abbreviated from his source.

2) In the context of the assassination of Philip II the term that is used to describe Pausanias at both Diodorus 16.93.3 and 16.93.9 is *somatophylax of the king*. In the eyes of the advocates of ambivalent terminology this means that he was among a group of *hypaspists* on guard duty as *doryphoroi* at the festival. *Doryphoroi* are indeed mentioned as being in the background in the theatre when Pausanias slew Philip, but Pausanias is obviously not one of them. If he had been, he would not have needed to conceal a dagger beneath his cloak, but would have been better armed. In the same context, Leonnatus, Perdiccas and Attalus are called *somatophylakes*, when they pursue and kill Pausanias. Yet at this time Leonnatus at least cannot easily be one of the seven elite Bodyguards of Philip, for he was only appointed as one of the king's elite Bodyguards much later under Alexander, replacing Aryhbas, who died of illness in Egypt (Arrian, *Anabasis* 3.5.5). But there is a simple solution: Alexander as Crown Prince must have had a set of personal bodyguards as well as Philip. It would be fitting for Leonnatus to have been one such in 336BC. Actually, Diodorus speaks of two groups of bodyguards, one of which pursued Pausanias with the other staying by the king. This is usually interpreted as describing a splitting of the king's bodyguards into two groups, but perhaps it literally reflects the existence of two teams of bodyguards: one for the king and the other for the prince.

3) Diodorus 17.61.3 states that Hephaistion was *Hegemon of the Somatophylakes* (literally "Commander of the Bodyguards") at Gaugamela. The advocates of ambivalent terminology insist that this must mean that he led the Palace Regiment of the *Hypaspist* infantry, even though it is likely on general grounds that Hephaistion was a member of the Seven at that time. They say that the king himself was the commander of the seven elite Bodyguards, although this is nowhere stated in our sources and there is evidence of a gradation of rank among the Seven when Diodorus 16.93.9 says that Philip gave Pausanias a more senior position among them. A bigger problem for the *hypaspist* command is that Hephaistion is stated to have fought with Alexander and the Companions in an isolated cavalry engagement at

Gaugamela (Arrian, *Anabasis* 3.15.1-2), which is very hard to explain, if he commanded a regiment of infantry in that battle. He had previously commanded the Mediterranean fleet (Curtius 4.5.10), which would have been awkward, if his rank was more junior than many of its existing officers (if he had been commander of the Palace *Hypaspists*, he would have reported to Nicanor, Parmenion's son, who led the *Hypaspist* Brigade according to Arrian, *Anabasis* 3.21.8). Hephaistion is never otherwise given an explicit military rank in any source until after the fall of Philotas, which is perfectly explained if he was an elite *somatophylax* rather than an army officer. As Bosworth has noted, there is no evidence for any of the seven elite Bodyguards having had an army rank until after Gaugamela.[15] In summary, it appears that Alexander did not gradually elevate Hephaistion through the military hierarchy. Instead, Hephaistion was one of the seven elite Bodyguards from the beginning of Alexander's reign and he was the most senior among them by the time of Gaugamela.

In conclusion, although orthodoxy would have us regard *hypaspist* and *somatophylax* as interchangeable terms, thus creating a deep vein of ambiguity and confusion at the heart of our key sources, we are equally at liberty to regard this as an entirely modern misunderstanding, such that *somatophylax* always means a personal elite bodyguard of some senior individual (usually the king) and no *hypaspist* is ever called a *somatophylax*, even though many *hypaspists* served as *doryphoroi*. It is clear to me that the latter viewpoint constitutes the most straightforward interpretation of the evidence. As a matter of principle, confused terminology should not be read into ancient sources unless the evidence clearly dictates it: in other words, this is not just a matter of taste.

The Large Lacuna in Curtius

There is a vast lacuna in the manuscript tradition of Curtius, which corresponds roughly to the sections from the beginning of 13.17 to the middle of 13.44 in my reconstruction of Cleitarchus. This equates to about a third of the entire length of Cleitarchus' thirteenth book, but, fortunately, Diodorus is particularly full and detailed for many of the key events in this interval and some supplementation from Plutarch and Justin has been feasible. Nevertheless, it is likely that the accounts of the following events in my reconstruction are more compressed relative to the archetype that the rest of Book 13:

The induction of Persians into elite guards regiments; Alexander's reconciliation with the Macedonian troops; the arrival of Peucestes and his archers; funding the upbringing of the orphaned sons of the troops; the onward march through Karai, Sittacenê and Sambana; visiting the Kelones, an old Greek settlement; sightseeing in Bagistanê; the quarrel between Hephaistion and Eumenes; the visit to the Nesaean mares; Atropates' pretend Amazons;

---

[15] A B Bosworth, *Conquest & Empire*, Appendix C, Section IV, "The Structure of Command".

The Reconstruction Of Book 13 Of Cleitarchus

festivities at Ecbatana and the death of Hephaistion; digression on Leosthenes' preparations for war back in Greece; the campaign against the Cossaeans; the warning from the Chaldeans and how the Greek philosophers persuaded Alexander to enter Babylon anyway; audiences with the envoys; preparations for Hephaistion's funeral and reprise of his status in Alexander's affections; description of the pyre; sacrifices to Hephaistion as a demigod; the omen of the prisoner on the throne; going astray in the marshes and the omen of the snagged diadem; Alexander falls ill at the party hosted by Medius; the doomed Alexander allows the troops to file past his sick-bed.

Hephaistion's Pyre

The Cleitarchan account of Hephaistion's pyre at Babylon must mainly be derived from Diodorus 17.115, which is anyway by far the most detailed description in any source. However, other ancient writers also alluded to its magnificence, novelty and exceptional cost: in the Cleitarchan sources this amounted to 12,000 talents, although this perhaps included the subsequent erection of a permanent memorial. A silver talent constituted 6000 drachms, each weighing ~4.2g, so this sum exceeded 300 tonnes of silver, equivalent to about 25 tonnes of gold in Alexander's day. Arrian and Plutarch give a figure of 10,000 talents, which is not seriously divergent, but which may indicate that they employed a source other than Cleitarchus on this point.

Plutarch, *Alexander* 72.3, adds that Alexander desired that Stasicrates should be its architect. This seems to be the same man who is elsewhere attributed with having restored the Temple of Artemis at Ephesus, designed Alexandria in Egypt and proposed a plan to carve Mt Athos in Thrace into a giant representation of Alexander with an entire city nestling in his left palm, although this last concept was rejected by Alexander. Whereas the name Stasicrates has the literal meaning of "one who triumphs over strife", he is elsewhere called Deinocrates (Vitruvius, *De architectura* 2, *praefatio* 1-4; Valerius Maximus 1.4 ext 1), which means "Master of Marvels" or Cheirocrates (Strabo 14.1.23), which is "Master of Hand-Skills": these apt appellations were presumably nicknames or possibly honorific titles.

Diodorus describes a structure erected upon a base of bricks a stade (=400 cubits) square and supporting itself upon palm trunks with the bricks having been gleaned by demolishing a ten-stade stretch of the city wall. He states that it comprised precisely thirty quadrangular chambers and that its exterior faces were decorated in six horizontal bands with the addition of an array of sirens hollowed out to accommodate human singers at its summit, which reached a height of 130 cubits.

Unfortunately, the precise form of this structure is not instantly unveiled by Diodorus' words. The matter of the configuration of the thirty chambers is especially obscure. C. Bradford Welles in the Loeb translation of Diodorus 17 suggests 30 transverse compartments each 22 feet wide and 220 yards long. Some have supposed that this edifice was a box-like tower with sheer sides, but major pyres are normally stepped pyramidal structures in Roman art. For example, they feature on coins, notably a denarius of Antoninus Pius. Furthermore, the stability of a simple rectangular structure a stade wide and 130 cubits tall that was entirely constructed of wood is dubious, for the force exerted upon its windward side in even a moderate breeze would have been tremendous. It might also be inferred that Stasicrates' inspiration was the ziggurat in Babylon, which probably also had seven pseudo-step-pyramidal stages. This concept is illustrated in the reconstruction of the pyre in the late 19th century engraving reproduced as Figure 2.2, where Hephaistion's pyre echoes the ziggurat depicted on the horizon of the panorama.

The solution to the conundrum probably lies in the geometrical significance of the number thirty, for $30=4x4+3x3+2x2+1x1$. Hence a square pyramidal structure comprising a four by four array of sixteen chambers on its foundation course, three by three on it first storey, two by two on its second and a single chamber at the summit precisely fits the description. This arrangement is illustrated in Figure 13.2 (p. 64), which shows that this suggests that each chamber measured 100x100x30 cubits, assuming that the final 10 cubits of height were provided by a plinth for the corpse. Diodorus' ensuing description of the decoration would be congruent with two bands per storey, excepting the topmost, where the sirens would have the full height of the crowning chamber. It is a strong confirmation of the width of the individual bands of decoration that Diodorus specified the overall height of the torches in the second frieze as fifteen cubits. The lower band of decoration on each storey might well have been projected outwards so as to give the impression of seven steps. Such projection might incidentally be helpful in accommodating the large reported total of sixty quinquireme prows per side at the base level of the decoration.

It is interesting to examine the iconography of the decorations in some detail, so I shall proceed from the base to the summit in the given order beginning with the galley prows in the first band. It is stated that each had a pair of archers on its catheads and five cubit tall fighting men on its deck. Olga Palagia has speculated that these vessels might represent Hephaistion's command of Alexander's Mediterranean fleet in 332BC (Curtius 4.5.10) and has noted that ships readied for a naval battle also appeared in the fourth decorative tablet on Alexander's funeral carriage (Diodorus 18.27.1).[16] But in fact the clue to decipherment of the symbolism probably lies again in the number of prows, for there were precisely sixty on each side of the structure, which matches the "sixty fighting ships" with which Alexander sailed across the Hellespont (Diodorus 17.17.2).[17] Hence we may infer that the armed men whom Diodorus notes to

---

[16] Olga Palagia, *Hephaestion's Pyre and the Royal Hunt of Alexander*, pp. 167-206 in "Alexander the Great in Fact and Fiction", edited by A. B. Bosworth & E. J. Baynham, Oxford, 2000.

[17] Probably this was only a section of Alexander's total fleet at the time, for Arrian, *Anabasis* 1.11.6 gives 160 triremes, Justin 11.6.2 has 182 ships and Curtius 4.5.14 gives Alexander a fleet of 160 vessels a couple of years later; indeed, Arrian's account states that Parmenion led the main

have been standing in each prow were probably actually Alexander and Hephaistion, with the former in the act of casting the famous spear, whereby Asia was won (see also Justin 11.5.10). Certainly Hephaistion was a key participant in the ensuing ceremonies at Troy itself, where he played Patrocles to Alexander's Achilles (Aelian, *Varia Historia* 12.7; Arrian, *Anabasis* 1.12.1). In fact Alexander's ceremonial crossing of the Hellespont looks very much like a re-enactment of the arrival of Achilles and Patrocles at Troy with the fifty ships that Homer attributed to the Myrmidons (Iliad 2.685).

Figure 2.2. Reconstruction of Hephaistion's Pyre by F. Jaffé (late 19th century – Author's Collection)

On the second level there were arrayed flaming torches with a serpent wound about each of their hafts, which gazed up at an eagle ascending from the flames. It is hard not to see the torch itself as symbolic of Hephaistion, because he was named for the Greek fire god, Hephaistos. According to Herodotus 8.98.2 the Greeks (e.g. the Athenians) held torch races in honour of Hephaistos. Notably, Hephaistion himself bore a torch in a named representation of the Chiliarch in a lost painting by Aetion (Figure 2.3), of which a detailed description has been preserved by Lucian (*Herodotus sive Aetion* 4-7). This explains exactly why each torch was wreathed, since the wreath was explicitly placed upon the badge of Hephaistion. The serpent and eagle are strongly associated with Ammon and

---

crossing from Sestus to Abydos, whereas Alexander crossed from Elaeus at the tip of the Hellespont directly opposite Troy nearly thirty km further south.

Zeus respectively, but they might also represent Alexander himself insofar as he had been publicly recognized as the son of Zeus-Ammon. Perhaps the tableau could be interpreted as Hephaistion acting as a support and inspiration to Alexander. We should expect to find such special and personal compliments to the deceased from the king in the iconography of the decoration of the pyre.

Figure 2.3. The Marriage of Alexander and Roxane by Sodoma, based upon the description by Lucian of a painting by Aetion and depicting Hephaistion bearing a torch (19th century engraving from the Author's Collection)

Regarding the hunting scene on the third tier of decoration, a fairly direct parallel survives in the hunt depicted on one of the long sides of the Alexander Sarcophagus found in the royal cemetery of Sidon in 1887 (Figure 2.4). This truly wondrous work of art appears to have been the tomb of Abdalonymus, who had been appointed king of Sidon by Alexander on the recommendation of Hephaistion (e.g. Curtius 4.1.15-20). In the hunting scene the rider behind the lion may be Hephaistion; the mounted man being attacked by the lion may be Abdalonymus and the third horseman may be Alexander, since he wore a diadem. In all probability the hunting scenes on the pyre were also an opportunity to commemorate the prowess and dynamism of the deceased in the chase as well as his camaraderie with his king in such pursuits.

The fourth band depicted a Centauromachy or fight of the Centaurs, which refers to the mythological battle between the Lapiths and the Centaurs. Its most renowned precedent was the Centauromachy shown in the metopes of the Parthenon in Athens, which Alexander would have visited in 338BC after the Battle of Chaeronea, probably in the company of Hephaistion. It is generally considered that the mythical Centauromachy often served to symbolize the struggle between the Greeks and the Persians, which is the most likely explanation for its inclusion on Hephaistion's pyre.

The Reconstruction Of Book 13 Of Cleitarchus

Fig. 2.4. The hunting scene on one of the long sides of the Alexander Sarcophagus from Sidon (from an albumen photo of the late 19th century in the Author's Collection).

The alternating bulls and lions in the fifth tier of adornment strongly recall the glazed brick reliefs of the Ishtar Gate and the adjoining Processional Way in Babylon, which were recovered by the German archaeological expeditions of Robert Koldewey in the early 20th century and used for a reconstruction displayed in the Pergamon Museum in Berlin. Alexander would certainly have seen them virtually every day he was in Babylon. The lions represent the goddess Ishtar and the bulls (technically aurochs) symbolize the god Adad. In the Babylonian Pantheon Ishtar was the goddess of love and war, whilst Adad was the god of storms. Lions also stood either side of the doorway of Alexander's catafalque, which was constructed in Babylon a little after the pyre (Diodorus 18.27.1). Similarly, a group of lions guarded one of the entrances to Alexander's probable first tomb at the Memphite Serapeum.[18] The main function of that temple was to house the mummified Apis Bulls in the famous subterranean galleries. Lion and bull motifs are also prominent in the decoration of other early Hellenistic tombs, such as, for example, Tomb No. 69 at Myra, which has a lion attacking a bull in the pediment of its façade.

A yet more widespread element of Greek funerary iconography was the panoply of arms, of which a fine example formed the sixth tier of ornamention on Hephaistion's pyre. There are numerous surviving parallels in Hellenistic artworks from tombs and mausoleums. An interesting example with which I myself have had some involvement is the starburst shield sculpture discovered embedded in the foundations of the main apse of the Basilica di San Marco in Venice (Figure 2.5). In the course of associating the sculpture with a Macedonian tomb, Eugenio Polito suggested in 1998 that the spear shaft extending to the upper lefthand corner of the front face of this block is a sarissa. He did not explain his reasoning, but it may be noted that the point of the spearhead appears to extend precisely to the square upper lefthand corner, which is an original corner. Obviously the corners on the righthand edge of the

---

[18] See *The Quest for the Tomb of Alexander the Great*, Andrew Chugg, 2007, pp. 62-66 & 134-145 (especially p.143).

block are not original, since it has been fractured away from another part on this side. However, symmetry arguments would suggest that the spear shaft should have terminated at the original bottom righthand corner. The scale of the other arms shows that the intention of the sculptor was to depict them all at precisely lifesize: for example, the shield appears to be a lifesize phalangite type (diameter 70cm). If so, then the spear-shaft was around three metres in length both in art and reality, which is about correct for a Macedonian cavalry sarissa or xyston. Alexander himself wields such a weapon in the mosaic depicting his charge against Darius at Issus, which was found in Pompeii and is now in the Naples Museum.

The spearhead on the block in Venice is rather similar to a spearhead discovered in a warrior grave at Aegae together with a connector circlet and a sauroter. These elements are believed to be the remains of the inorganic parts of a sarissa comprising two wooden shafts joined by the connector with a spike at one end and a leaf-shaped spearhead at the other.

The sculpture also depicts a pair of greaves in high relief, although they are now badly damaged. They are staggered in height on the block just to the right of the shield and the individual greaves are to scale: the bottom of the upper greave is at approximately the level of the lowest part of the star design on the shield. There is also a *kopis*, a single-edged hacking sword popular with Alexander's troops, which is suspended from a taselled belt on the lefthand side and is also precisely lifesize in scale. Its surface has however been seriously abraded.

Eugenio Polito assumed that the block had been imported to Venice from "the Eastern Mediterranean" and dated it to the third or early second century BC. It is sculpted from late Cretaceous limestone with rudist fossils, which may be found in the Roman Aurisina quarry seventy miles from Venice or in the vicinity of the lost pyramid at Abu Roash on the Nile, which was destroyed to provide sculptural stone in Ptolemaic Egypt.

The starburst design embossed upon the shield is perhaps its most striking feature, redolent as it is of the starburst emblem of the Macedonian monarchy, most famously emblazoned upon the lid of the larnax that held the cremated bones of King Philip of Macedon in Tomb II at Aegae. Starburst shields like this one appear on Macedonian coins and in several Macedonian wall paintings, notably in a mural depicting a Macedonian panoply in the tomb of Lyson & Kallikles located within Macedon itself. Phalangite and hoplite shields are commonly interspersed on Macedonian monuments.[19] A pair of rimless phalangite shields are depicted either side of the entrance on the façade of Tomb III at Aegae, which is probably the tomb of Alexander's son, Alexander IV, in which case it will have been constructed at the beginning of the third century BC.

---

[19] See "A Shield Monument from Veria and the Chronology of Macedonian Shield Types", Minor Markle, *Hesperia* 68.2, 1999.

The Reconstruction Of Book 13 Of Cleitarchus

In practice, the trophy of arms motif was the core symbolism for the tomb of a Macedonian warrior. It was roughly the equivalent of a cross on a Christian grave. Here is a contemporaneous quotation that makes the point:

It is fitting for the Macedonian spirit to bear witness to exploits with arms in fighting, and to fairness of the soul, so that trophies may proclaim the valour of the body, but opinions may testify to the soul's nobility.

FrGrHist 2.153 F4 = Freiburg Papyrus 7-8

Therefore, this kind of symbolism is what an expert would expect to find in closest association with the corpse of a Macedonian notable, so it is no surprise to read that trophies of arms formed the penultimate band of decoration on Hephaistion's pyre.

At the summit of the pyre there stood statues of Sirens that had been hollowed out to accommodate human singers. Clearly, there is a allusion to the Sirens of Homer's Odyssey with their impossibly lovely yet baleful voices. Only the most movingly mournful laments could be deemed worthy of the deceased. It is worth noticing that effigies of Sirens were also found among the statuary near Alexander's probable first tomb at the Serapeum in the Memphite necropolis at Saqqara: it is most likely that these were set up by Ptolemy Soter, who was undoubtedly an eyewitness at Hephaistion's funeral.

The archaeologist Robert Koldewey located a possible site for Hephaistion's pyre during his excavations of Babylon in the early 20th century (see plan on page 45). He uncovered a scorched and reddened platform beneath a mound of brick rubble close to the inner wall of Babylon due east of the "Southern Palace" of Nebuchadnezzar.[20] Koldewey even described having found the imprints of incinerated palm trunks on the platform, recalling Diodorus' description quite evocatively.

It seems likely that it was Alexander's intention to build a mausoleum echoing the architecture of the pyre in its ashes, although this was thwarted by the king's premature demise. Among the Last Plans of Alexander, which are outlined in Diodorus 18.4 based on documents read to the Assembly of the Macedones by Perdiccas, there was an item calling for the "completion of the pyre of Hephaistion" at great expense. It is important to understand that in Greek the term used, which is *pyra*, can mean either a funeral pyre or a temple altar (i.e. a place where fire is kindled). Hence it can reasonably be used to refer both to the incinerated pyre and the altar of a permanent memorial, where a flame was to be kept alight for the Chiliarch. There is evidence for permanent memorials having been erected upon the cinders of funeral pyres in the case of other major Macedonian tombs: for example, a monument from the late 4th century BC has

---

[20] See "Hephaestion's Pyre and the Royal Hunt of Alexander" by Olga Palagia in *Alexander the Great in Fact and Fiction*, edited by A. B. Bosworth and E. J. Baynham, Oxford 2000, p. 173; R. Koldewey, *The Excavations at Babylon*, London 1914, p. 310-11.

been excavated at Salamis on the coast of Cyprus, where a funeral pyre had been built upon a brick platform and a stone pyramid was subsequently erected in its place as a permanent memorial – this may be associated with the naval battle at Salamis between Ptolemy and Demetrius Poliorcetes in 306BC.[21]

Figure 2.5. Macedonian arms sculpted upon two faces of a block from the foundations of the Basilica di San Marco in Venice (photo by the author.)

---

[21] Plutarch, *Demetrius* 17.1; V. Karageorghis, *Cyprus*, London, 1969, pp. 171-199.

The Reconstruction Of Book 13 Of Cleitarchus

Hephaistion the Demigod

The manuscripts of Diodorus had Alexander decree that Hephaistion should receive sacrifices as *theos proedros*, but this is corrected to *theos paredros* on the basis of Lucian, *Calumniae non temere credendum* 17, which speaks of sacrifices to Hephaistion as *paredros kai alexikakos theos* (assistant and guardian divinity); this use of *paredros*, which literally means "one who sits beside" (as opposed to *proedros*, which means "sitting in front of"), is unusual and in this context seems to mean an assistant god or collaborating deity, which is not greatly inconsistent with the versions of Arrian, *Anabasis* 7.23.6 and Plutarch, *Alexander* 72.2, which state that Ammon approved the honouring of Hephaistion as a hero. Perhaps the very oddity of *paredros* is suggestive of authentic terminology. The only surviving named portrait of Hephaistion from antiquity is a stele from Thessalonike in Macedonia, which depicts him standing beside a horse with a libation being poured by a woman into a bowl that he holds out (Figure 2.6). It bears a dedicatory inscription from a certain Diogenes to the hero Hephaistion (*DIOGENES HEPHAISTIONI HEROI*). Hence it probably represents a tangible consequence of the semi-divine status accorded to Hephaistion by the Oracle of Ammon.

Figure 2.6. Stele from Thessalonike dedicated to the hero Hephaistion (sketch by the author).

The Death of Alexander the Great by Andrew Chugg

The Cause of the Death of Alexander

There are three main causes for Alexander's premature demise for which significant evidence is attested by the ancient sources:

1) Excessive indulgence in alcohol
2) A feverish illness
3) Poisoning by Iollas at the instigation of Antipater

Cleitarchus seems to have been aware of the controversy, but to have had no firm favourite among them. Instead he chose to present evidence for all three. Thus he mentioned (13.43 below) that Alexander's Friends had spread the word that the onset of his fatal illness had been caused by drinking too much wine. But his actual description of the illness is highly reminiscent of escalating disease symptoms, especially since it agrees with other sources in stretching the duration of the sickness over a week or more. The Iollas poisoning theory is then related as an addendum to the description of the events themselves (13.84 below) with a noncommittal introduction from our author, which verges on a disclaimer. Cleitarchus' description of the plot follows the conspiracy described in the *Liber de Morte* section of the Metz Epitome (87-123) in some detail, so it would seem that Cleitarchus had read its notorious source pamphlet, yet had not been convinced by its assertions.

Although I recognize that the true cause of Alexander's death remains controversial to this day, I have argued in *The Quest for the Tomb of Alexander the Great* that the ancient evidence in fact presents an overwhelming probabilistic case for death through infection by the most deadly strain of malaria. It is apposite to reprise the case in summary with a view to showing that the version of events given by Cleitarchus is not at all inconsistent with this diagnosis.

Of key significance is Alexander's expedition through the marshes just a week or two before he fell ill. Falciparum malaria has been endemic to the Mesopotamian marshes through to modern times. The local population always acquires a degree of resistance to such deadly diseases, but they are especially pernicious for newcomers to an infected region. When its prevalence is combined with its dire deadliness, this is overwhelmingly the most perilous threat from a feverish disease to which Alexander was exposed. The statistical argument is virtually decisive in isolation, for death by this strain of malaria is literally thousands of times more probable than such other rare and exotic syndromes as have been contrived to fit the evidence: for example, the typhoid theory with the rare complication of ascending paralysis and coma, as proposed by Oldach & Richards (*New England Journal of Medicine*, 11th June 1998).

But we need not rely upon statistics, since the interval between the marshes and the famous party at which Alexander collapsed is precisely consistent with the incubation period for falciparum malaria. This disease also has a characteristic and pronounced pattern of fever peaks, for it presents as a quotidian fever, which means that it has a twenty-four hour cycle of peaks and troughs. In the first few days the fever will virtually vanish at one time of day and yet rage mercilessly twelve hours later. As the disease progresses the hatchings of broods of the parasite that are responsible for stimulating these fever bouts start to overlap and the fever rages more continuously. Hence we should expect a pronounced intermittency of Alexander's fever in its initial stages and indeed there is no difficulty in finding evidence of this in the accounts of Plutarch and Arrian, both of which are stated to have been based of Alexander's own journal, kept by Eumenes his secretary and known as the *Ephemerides*. We read of a fever raging though the nights, whereas the king long continued to conduct normal matters of business during daylight hours. After four or five days Arrian explicitly states that Alexander "no longer had any rest from the fever", which shows that he had experienced marked remissions up to that point.

The onset of the illness is most comprehensively described in the Cleitarchan sources, which speak of Alexander experiencing stabbing pains in his back and all over his body after quaffing a large beaker of wine at Medius' party. It is ironic that the Cleitarchan authors believed that they were relating evidence of poisoning, when in fact just such stabbing pains in the limb joints and between the vertebrae of the spine are typical of the onset of falciparum malaria. Furthermore, there are clear indications of a profound terminal coma in the fresh and lifelike appearance of the corpse reported by Curtius 10.10.12-13 and Plutarch, *Alexander* 77.3 some days after the pronouncement of death. Cerebral malaria leading to terminal coma is absolutely the normal outcome in untreated cases of falciparum malaria among newcomers to the region of infection. We even have the detail deriving from Aristobulus that Alexander became delirious before the end, which is perfectly congruent with the onset of cerebral malaria (although Aristobulus sought to explain it as a consequence of Alexander having drunk some wine.) Falciparum malaria will also progressively attack a range of organs including the lungs, which readily explains the weakness of Alexander's voice, which is recalled by several sources, including Justin 12.15.12 from among the Cleitarchan authors. Even the least of Alexander's symptoms – e.g. indications of a weak appetite in that he is said to have been eating "lightly" – are consistent with malaria. I know of no recorded symptom that is at all inconsistent with malaria and overall Alexander's demise is a near casebook account of a falciparum malaria fatality.

In summary, there is an immensely strong case for falciparum malaria in the reported evidence. It seems to be the only statistically credible explanation that is not contradicted by any evidence from any of the ancient sources. Perhaps the most impressive point in its favour is that it happily reconciles the supposed poisoning symptoms reported by the Vulgate sources (including Cleitarchus) with the sober description of death through an escalating feverish disease from the Ephemerides. In fact the onset of falciparum malaria in its standard case history would have looked very much like a case of poisoning to any ancient observer with a less than thorough familiarity with the finer points of tropical medicine.

Yet the fact that death occurred more than a week after the supposed poisoning symptoms actually renders poisoning highly improbable, for the simple reason that any poison capable of producing such a dramatic reaction should have killed Alexander right away. It is almost impossible that he should have lingered for ten days before dying, unless there had been repeated applications of the drug. The *Liber de Morte* author (Holcias?) seems implicitly to have recognized this in formulating the story of a poisoned feather used to repeat the dosing at a late stage in Alexander's illness. Although it may be allowed that feathers were used in antique medicine to induce vomiting, this story is very hard to swallow (please excuse any perceived pun). Neither the concept of Alexander gulping a sticky or dripping wet feather nor the idea that something intended to bring poison up would have seemed a good way of getting it down makes any sense.

One modern attempt to rescue the poisoning theory has been to suppose the "Styx water in a mule's hoof" to have been actual water contaminated by some biological disease, but this would not of course have produced any of the prompt poisoning symptoms reported at Medius' party. It also ascribes quite a detailed practical knowledge of bacterial biology to the putative poisoner, which is equally dubious.

It is not feasible to be absolutely certain of the cause of Alexander's death unless and until a post mortem is performed upon his remains. However, it is impossible that the tight fit between the case history in our sources and the contraction and progression of a case of falciparum malaria could have been forged. Even if such a fit did not exist, the mere fact that Alexander had visited the Babylonian marshes a few weeks before his death would be sufficient to make falciparum malaria statistically its most likely cause.

How Did the Leading Men Split after Alexander's Death?

A dramatic explosion of factional politics dominates the picture that Cleitarchus seems to have painted of the situation at Babylon in the immediate aftermath of Alexander's death. Yet in principle the pecking order among the senior men was relatively clear. In particular, the seven or eight *somatophylakes* of the king stood at the apex of the court hierarchy and held many of the most senior army commands. Furthermore, they were all Macedonians, which gave them a crucial advantage over the broader elite of the king's Friends comprising around fifty men, of whom at least a third were not Macedonians. Since the ultimate power to acclaim a new king was vested in the Assembly of the Macedonian troops, narrow nationalistic considerations suddenly came swingeing to the fore.

The *somatophylakes* at Babylon in June 323BC were: Perdiccas of Orestis, Leonnatus of Pella & Lyncestis, Aristonous of Eordaea & Pella, Pithon of Alcomenae, Peucestes of Mieza, Lysimachus of Pella & Crannon in Thessaly

The Reconstruction Of Book 13 Of Cleitarchus

and Ptolemy of Eordaea. Seleucus of Europus, probably the commander of the Silver Shields (*argyraspides* - formerly the hypaspists) may have been an eighth, assuming that the vacancy created by the death of Hephaistion had been filled. Among these officers, Perdiccas seems to have enjoyed acknowledged pre-eminence: he was evidently the most senior *somatophylax* and Alexander had been seen to hand him his signet ring.

There additionally survives an explicit list of the key men in Babylon at Alexander's death as preserved in the opening section of Photius' Epitome of Arrian's *Events after Alexander*. It states that Perdiccas, Leonnatus and Ptolemy were the top-ranking cavalry officers, whereas Lysimachus, Aristonous, Pithon, Seleucus and Eumenes were cavalry officers of the second rank. It also notes that Meleager led the infantry faction, which is amply corroborated in my reconstruction of Cleitarchus.

Curtius, probably following Cleitarchus, provides us with a profound insight into the lines along which opinions and sentiments were divided among the *somatophylakes* as they met to discuss the future without Alexander. It is particularly striking that *somatophylakes* from the eastern cantons and townships of Macedonia (Orestis, Lyncestis, Eordaea and Alcomenae) lined up volubly behind Perdiccas, for Leonnatus, Aristonous and Pithon explicitly supported him in the Cleitarchan account. The only exception was Ptolemy of Eordaea, but he was probably only an Eordaean by adoption[22] and he anyway soon reverted to supporting Perdiccas' cause, when his own proposals were seen to lack significant backing and the cavalry faction as a whole united in the face of Meleager's abortive attempt to seize power in the name of Philip-Arrhidaeus. Justin further suggests that Attalus supported Meleager. If so, the former managed somehow to make his peace with the cavalry *hipparchs* before or after Meleager's fall, since he did not share in Meleager's fate. It is possible that he was estranged from Meleager by the offer of the hand of Perdiccas' sister Atalante, since Diodorus 18.37.2 later names her as hs wife. He subsequently led the pursuit of Alexander's catafalque on behalf of Perdiccas, when Ptolemy had diverted it towards Egypt.

The position of Nearchus of Amphipolis & Crete is intriguing. He evidently chose to espouse the cause of Alexander's illegitimate son by Barsine, probably because he had married a daughter of Barsine at Susa the previous year. Unsurprisingly, advocacy of Heracles proved politically unpopular among the Macedonians, so Nearchus merely managed to isolate himself. This may be reflected in the fact that, despite his eminence under Alexander, he was not awarded outright control of any territory in the First Division of the Satrapies,

---

[22] He seems to have been an illegitimate son of Philip II, who was adopted by Lagus, when the latter married his mother Arsinoe: Pausanias 1.6.2; Curtius 9.8.22; *Armenian Alexander Romance* 269; Plutarch, *Moralia* 458A-B; *Suidae Lexicon* s.v. Lagos..

although he may have been appointed as a deputy to Antigonus in Lycia and Pamphylia.

Eumenes of Cardia does not have any prominent role in the Cleitarchan version of events at Babylon, although he had inherited Perdiccas' hipparchy of the Companion Cavalry after the death of Hephaistion (Plutarch, *Eumenes* 1.5; Nepos, *Eumenes* 1.6). However, Plutarch, *Eumenes* 3.2 states that he stayed in Babylon maintaining neutrality, when the other cavalry officers went out into the surrounding countryside and that he was thereafter influential in persuading the infantry to reach an accommodation with Perdiccas.[23]

The stance of the other *somatophylakes* (Lysimachus, Peucestes and perhaps Seleucus) is not explicitly stated by our sources, but their backing for Perdiccas may be inferred from the fact that they all received important and desirable appointments in the First Division of the Satrapies.

Considering that Perdiccas enjoyed such broad support among the elite men, it is remarkable that the infantry managed to cause him so much trouble. The Cleitarchan analysis was that he did well in making a show of giving up Alexander's ring at the crucial meeting in the aftermath of Alexander's death, but that he was too hesitant in retrieving it, when the meeting had been rallied behind him by his supporters, thereby ceding the troublemakers their opportunity. I find this a rather compelling human explanation of the events, which is not significantly contradicted by any other account, although no other version provides anything approaching the same degree of detail.

Arrhidaeus the Fool

There is virtual unanimity among the ancient sources on the fact that Arrhidaeus suffered from some form of mental impairment. Plutarch, *Alexander* 77.7-8 even goes so far as to allege that this had resulted from a drug administered to him by Olympias in his childhood. One of the most explicit references on this matter is the Heidelberg Epitome 1-2, which states:

"When Alexander died, he left behind his wives and an unborn son by Roxane. His followers quarrelled about who should become king, but Alexander's half-brother Arrhidaeus, who was later called Philip, was appointed king until the son of Alexander reached an appropriate age. Because Arrhidaeus was dull-witted and also epileptic, Perdiccas was appointed to be guardian and overseer of the royal government."

There are further attestations of Arrhidaeus' affliction in: Plutarch, *Alexander* 10.2 & 77.7-8; Diodorus 18.2; Justin 13.2.11 & 14.5.2. Justin 13.2.11 (backed up by Diodorus) is the sources for the mention of Arrhidaeus' incapacity in the reconstruction of Cleitarchus at 13.61. Curtius appears to have edited out the

---

[23] Jane Hornblower, *Hieronymus of Cardia*, p.88, thinks Plutarch used Hieronymus on Eumenes.

hostile invective, probably because he was drawing a parallel with the accession of his own emperor, Claudius. The ensemble of evidence on Philip-Arrhidaeus and especially the lack of any contrary indications from any ancient source leave little room for doubt that he was conspicuously sub-normal. Thus it would be appropriate to read a certain element of disingenuousness into the advocacy of Arrhidaeus' succession by Meleager and his cronies.

Plutarch, *Alexander* 10.2, has Alexander describe Arrhidaeus literally as a bastard in the context of the Pixodarus affair. However, some have supposed that Philip's attempt to marry off Arrhidaeus to the eldest daughter of Pixodarus, the satrap of Caria, in the cause of recruiting him as an ally must mean that Philip had married Arrhidaeus' mother, Philinna, since Arrhidaeus must have had the status of a legitimate son to be an acceptable groom. This relies on a Christian concept of illegitimacy as a sanction against indulgence in sex outside of marriage, which is of course a way of thinking that would have been utterly alien in the Greek world of the 4th century BC. Instead, the social function of illegitimacy for the Greeks was as a legal device to inhibit the division and disintegration of the assets and estates of wealthy families among the many illegitimate offspring sired by their senior male members. Consequently, the emphasis in deciding your legitimacy status in that culture does not seem to have been on whether your father had married your mother (although legitimacy was automatic and implicit, if he had), but rather on whether your father had publicly acknowledged you as his son or daughter.

It is likely that Philip had to acknowledge Arrhidaeus as his own in order to make a marriage with Pixodarus' daughter viable, but he did not need to have married Philinna: the quote of Alexander from Plutarch strongly suggests that he had not; also Satyrus (Athenaeus 13.5 [557C]) states that Philip fathered Arrhidaeus on Philinna, but conspicuously avoids saying that he married her. However, the official acknowledgement of Arrhidaeus explains why the troops were so ready to accept his claim to the throne in Babylon, despite his mother having been an unmarried dancing girl from Larissa. It also explains just why the Pixodarus marriage so upset Alexander: his bastard half-brother was now his official half-brother through this marriage, thereby becoming a theoretical threat to Alexander's succession. Philip probably calculated that Arrhidaeus' impaired mental faculties guaranteed that the threat to Alexander would remain hypothetical, but Alexander could not afford to feel so relaxed about the matter, for Arrhidaeus could yet be played as a pawn against him. Events after Alexander's death show that Alexander was right to fear the consequences of Arrhidaeus being adopted by a faction as a puppet king and that Philip miscalculated the risks of legitimizing an imbecile into the official Royal Family.

The First Division of the Satrapies

The reapportionment of control of the satrapies of Alexander's Empire effectuated by Perdiccas in June of 323BC at Babylon survives in three main traditions that I will term the Photian, the Cleitarchan and the Metz. The first derives from Photius' summaries of Dexippus and of Arrian's lost work on *Events After Alexander*. Secondly, each of Curtius, Diodorus and Justin cite lists that appear to preserve the version from Cleitarchus. Finally, the *Liber de Morte* section at the end of the Metz Epitome has a variant of the list, which it attributes to the spurious *Will of Alexander*, but which nevertheless generally encapsulates the outcome of the Perdiccan division. Some parts of the Metz tradition also appear in Pseudo-Callisthenes, although in an even more garbled form. The Cleitarchan tradition is summarized in Table 2.2, including my reconstruction of Cleitarchus himself in its final column; whereas the Photian and Metz versions are cited for comparison in Table 2.3, which also incorporates a version of the Second Division that was implemented by Antipater a few years later, the latter also being abstracted from Photius' summary of Arrian.

It is initially striking how much agreement there is to be found between these disparate sources. Once allowance has been made for various errors of transcription and transliteration, there is a great deal of commonality between them all. Particularly intricate details are shared by the Photian and Cleitarchan traditions: for example, both apparently mentioned that Eumenes' remit should extend specifically to the town of Trapezus (Trebizond) on the Euxine Sea; furthermore, the satrapies are dealt with in a similar order in each case and the eastern section is prefixed with the observation that its existing satraps were generally allowed to remain in office. These commonalities strongly suggest that all these traditions had their origins in a single contemporaneous, archetypal document.

Nevertheless, a focussed review of aberrant details of the First Division may help assuage the doubts aired by some, such as N. G. L. Hammond, as to whether the vivid, blow-by-blow account of the succession of Philip III in the latter half of the tenth book of Curtius is actually derived from Cleitarchus. In general, the differences between the traditions, though relatively few, bear close examination, because they may well serve to define the interpretation of the archetypal list by intermediary authors, notably Cleitarchus.

Perhaps the clearest instance is that the satrapy of Caria is awarded to Asander in the Photian lists, but consistently to Cassander in the Cleitarchan and also the Metz traditions. This was actually Asander the son of Agathon from Beroea, probably a relative of Antigonus, so we can say that there is a consistent error in the Cleitarchan version, which may therefore most credibly be traced back to the prototype variant of Cleitarchus. Certainly, the observation that Curtius, Diodorus and Justin all share in this error is a strong indication that they are all still following Cleitarchus at this point, despite the fact that the First Division occurred at an interval of a week or two after Alexander's death.

A second variation is that the reinstatement of Atropates as Satrap of Lesser Media seems only to be mentioned in Cleitarchan versions. He is cited among the examples of an existing eastern satrap, whose associations with the new

The Reconstruction Of Book 13 Of Cleitarchus

regime have enabled him to retain his position, even though the satrapy of Greater Media is assigned to Pithon in the first half of the list dealing with the western and central satrapies. In Justin, Atropates is noted to have retained Lesser Media as the "father-in-law of Perdiccas", a relationship that he had achieved through the Susa marriages of 324BC. The Photian tradition evidently omitted mention of Atropates, whereas Cleitarchus seemingly saw fit to draw attention to this evidence for the nature of the patronage dispensed by the Perdiccan regime.

It would also appear that the Cleitarchan list gave Seleucus command of the Companion Cavalry in the First Division, whereas both the Photian and Metz traditions granted him immediate governance of Babylonia. In fact, it seems that Seleucus was not given control of Babylonia until the Second Division and that the Cleitarchan tradtion correctly recalls that Archon of Pella initially received Babylonia. This shows that the Cleitarchan tradition is certainly no less accurate overall that the Photian sources: a case might even be made that the Cleitarchan in fact provides the most accurate and detailed surviving account.

There is a slight difference of emphasis between the Cleitarchan and Photian traditions in that the former asserts that Ptolemy was to replace Cleomenes, whereas the latter suggests that Cleomenes was to become Ptolemy's deputy. It is tempting to explain this as political correctness on Cleitarchus' part, since he is believed to have written in Egypt under Ptolemaic rule, where the first Ptolemy had actually executed Cleomenes. It certainly harmonises with the assumption that Cleitarchus is the source of First Division details in Curtius, Justin and Diodorus.

It is interesting that Justin uniquely assigned Nearchus as the Satrap of Lycia and Pamphylia. This has been considered an error influenced by Alexander's earlier award of these territories to Nearchus (Arrian, *Anabasis* 3.6.6). However, we do know that Nearchus was active in Pamphylia and southern Asia Minor in the years following Alexander's death (Polyaenus 5.35) and it is mildly strange that someone so eminent as Nearchus lacks any role elsewhere in the First Division. The alternative interpretation would be that Nearchus was indeed awarded his former satrapies in the First Division, but that he was also required to report to Antigonus in this capacity. Hence he acted as a deputy to Antigonus, who most ancient writers therefore recognized as the true ruler of Lycia and Pamphylia. Certainly, by 317-316BC Nearchus is explicitly operating as a lieutenant of Antigonus in leading a force of lightly armed troops into the Cossaean territory (Diodorus 19.19.4-5).

There is some additional evidence to be gleaned across the traditions that the archetypal source on the First Division recorded significant appointments in assistant or deputy posts against some of the satrapies and other high offices: as well as Cleomenes' status in Egypt, there is a sense in which Craterus is presented as Antipater's assistant in Europe. It is a possibility that Atropates was subordinate to Pithon in Media: perhaps it was only the nepotism interest that persuaded Cleitarchus to mention his appointment. In general, the surviving sources may have edited out much information on subordinate appointments in the cause of epitomizing a morass of data, which was to be found in the archetype.

There is huge scope for confusion in that two men named Pithon were awarded satrapies in the First Division and this problem was compounded by the fact that the Pithon who took Greater Media and was a Bodyguard of Alexander had a father named Crateuas, which is deceptively close to Craterus – hence in all probability the award of Greater Media to "Craterus" in the Metz version. The other Pithon was the son of Agenor and he seems to have been awarded control of those parts of India that did not fall within the domains of Taxiles and Porus. Pithon the son of Crateuas came from Alcomenae in Deuriopus[24] on the borders of Illyria, which probably explains why he is called "Illyrius" in Justin. This is likely to be the epithet employed by Cleitarchus to distinguish him from the son of Agenor. Unfortunately, some editors have instead interpreted this as a reference to the "satrapy" of Illyria. In fact the fate of Illyria seems only to be mentioned by the Photian tradition, which includes it among Antipater's territories, and the Metz Epitome, which assigns it to Holcias. The prominence of Holcias in the Metz has been held to suggest that he may have been the original author of the *Liber de Morte*. The indications that the original assignments extended to deputy roles would suggest that the archetype of the First Division list might have granted him subordinate control of Illyria reporting to Antipater. He is certainly a real historical character of some prominence, since he appears in Polyaenus 4.6.6 as one of the leaders of three thousand troops, who had revolted from Antigonus.

However, the key conclusion must be that Cleitarchus gave a well-informed and mostly accurate summary of the First Division of the Satrapies, which he probably abstracted from an archetypal published list. It subsequently became the basis for the surviving summaries in Diodorus, Curtius and Justin. The First Division was destined to have vast repercussions: it established the Ptolemaic Dynasty in Egypt and set Antigonus Monophthalmus and Seleucus Nicator upon their paths to glory. It also provided the model for successive divisions by Antipater at Triparadeisus (see also Diodorus 18.39.5-7) in 320BC and Antigonus in the aftermath of Gabiene (Diodorus 19.48) in 316BC.

Last Plans

Sections 13.81-83 of my reconstruction are derived exclusively from Diodorus 18.4.1-6 dealing with Alexander's "Last Plans": direct evidence for their ultimate derivation from Cleitarchus is weak, but all other material in Diodorus 18.1-4 seems to be Cleitarchan due to close and particular matches with Curtius and Justin. Hence it would appear Diodorus did not switch sources to Hieronymus

---

[24] Strabo 7.7.8.

The Reconstruction Of Book 13 Of Cleitarchus

of Cardia until 18.5.[25] The geographical review of Asia in Diodorus 18.5-6 is a strong indication of a switch to a new source, since such scene setting at the opening of their books was common among Hellenistic historians. For example, Cleitarchus himself seems to have given a geographical and cultural review of India by way of introduction to the tenth book of his work at the outset of Alexander's invasion of the sub-continent.

The fact that the genuineness of the Last Plans has so often been impugned[26] is arguably a clearer reflection of the sceptical loading of some scholars' scales rather than their balanced verdicts, for it can scarcely be deemed to mirror the weight of the evidence, which inclines towards authenticity. The key point is that nearly all of Alexander's plans as rejected by Perdiccas and the Assembly and which Diodorus lists as "memoranda" (*hypomnemata*) have close parallels in the actions and objectives of Alexander recorded elsewhere among our sources. Furthermore, there is copious evidence that an extensive body of Royal Papers existed, including also the journal known as the *Ephemerides* and the distances for stages in Alexander's marches, called the *Stathmoi* (see my paper on *The Journal of Alexander the Great* in *Ancient History Bulletin* 19.3-4, 2005 and reprinted in *The Quest*). It is hard to imagine that Perdiccas would have wished to invent spurious Plans merely to have them set aside by the Assembly and it is even harder to see how the existence of these Plans offered political advantage to any faction. In other words, forgery would have been a motiveless crime.

Let us consider the corroborative evidence for the individual plans:

1) Completion of the memorial altar of Hephaistion

> Plutarch, *Alexander* 72.3, reports essentially the same plan: "[Alexander] proposed to expend ten thousand talents upon a tomb (*tumbos*) and obsequies for his friend, wishing that the ingenuity and novelty of the construction should surpass the outlay." Arrian, *Anabasis* 7.14.8, concurs, even using the same ambiguous term as Diodorus: "[Alexander] ordered a pyre/altar to be made ready for [Hephaistion] at Babylon at a cost of ten thousand talents – by some accounts even more." The extraordinary expense mitigates in favour of a permanent memorial being envisaged in addition to a combusted funeral pyre.

2) A thousand warships larger than triremes to be built in Phoenicia, Syria, Cilicia and Cyprus for a campaign against Carthage

> According to Arrian, *Anabasis* 7.19.4, Alexander had recently assembled various fleets at Babylon for the purposes of the Arabian

---

[25] Jane Hornblower, *Hieronymus of Cardia*, pp.80-97, broadly supports the view that Cleitarchus was the source of the Last Plans and much of the other material in Diodorus 18.2-4 and she agrees that the geographical review comes from the opening of Hieronymus' account of the history of Alexander's successors.

[26] Perhaps most notably by W. W. Tarn, *Alexander the Great, Vol II: Sources & Studies*, p.378f.

circumnavigation in a harbour that he had dredged out to accommodate a thousand warships. That the whole space was needed is shown by Curtius 10.1.19, who records that 700 vessels were to be built at Thapsacus on the Euphrates to be sailed down to Babylon and added to Nearchus' fleet. It is an obvious corollary that the same size of fleet would have been required to support the North African campaign in the Mediterranean, since in Alexander's day there was no practicable sea-route to take the Arabian fleet into the Mediterranean. The campaign against the Carthaginians is also outlined by Curtius 10.1.17.

3) A road along the coast of North Africa as far as the Pillars of Heracles

The *Metz Epitome* 63 notes that Alexander planned ultimately to reach the Atlantic (in fact the manuscript read *adlanticum montem*, which might mean the Pillars of Heracles). Curtius 10.1.17 is explicit that Alexander wished to march to the Pillars of Heracles.

4) Six shrines at a cost of 1500 talents each to be set up at Delos, Delphi & Dodona in Greece and three in Macedonia: a temple of Zeus at Dium, of Tauropolus at Amphipolis[27] and of Athena at Cyrrhus[28]

This must have been among the written instructions given to Craterus, when he set off for Greece, for Plutarch, *Moralia* 343D, evidently cites the same programme of temple construction: "Alexander captured the riches of barbarians and sent them to Greece with orders that ten thousand talents be used to construct temples for the gods."

5) Ports and shipyards to be constructed to support Alexander's expeditions

Curtius 10.1.17-19 effectively corroborates Alexander's entire plan to march around the Mediterranean littoral in a clockwise direction starting from Syria. The practical need for suitable harbours and shipyards was an inevitable corollary.

6) To establish cities and to transfer populations from Asia to Europe and from Europe to Asia

There is copious evidence for Alexander's policy of settling Greeks in newly founded cities in Asia. For example, Polybius 10.27.3 writes: "Media is the most notable principality in Asia… On its borders a ring of Greek cities was founded by Alexander to protect it from the

---

[27] W. W. Tarn and also Russel M. Geer in the Loeb edition of Diodorus 18 make Tauropolus a manifestation of Artemis and there are some coins of Amphipolis with a goddess astride a bull; but Tauropolus the son of Dionysus and Ariadne is associated with the Thracian Chersonese and would seem an alternative possibility, given that Amphipolis lay near the Thracian border – but perhaps Tauropolus was manifested as the bull that Artemis rode.

[28] Cyrrhus is Cyrnus in the manuscripts, but it seems preferable to assume that the known Macedonian town is intended.

neighbouring barbarians." Then Pausanias 1.25.5 and 8.52.5 has: "All the Greeks who had served as mercenaries in the armies of Darius and his satraps Alexander had wished to deport to Persia, but Leosthenes was too quick for him, and brought them by sea to Europe... Leosthenes, in spite of Alexander's opposition, brought back safe by sea to Greece the force of Greek mercenaries in Persia, about fifty thousand in number, who had descended to the coast." Also Diodorus 17.99.5-6 states: "The Greeks who had been settled in Bactria and Sogdiana, who had long borne unhappily their sojourn among peoples of a different race, now received word that the king [Alexander] had died of his wounds and they revolted against the Macedonians. They formed a band of three thousand men and underwent great hardships on their homeward route." There is little evidence for the colonizing of Europe by Asiatic people, but this is mainly because the European campaigns had yet to happen at Alexander's death. We should have to suppose a radical shift of policy by Alexander, if he had no intention of founding cities and populating them with suitable groups from among his followers in the context of the forthcoming European expedition. Alexander probably believed that he was emulating his forebear, Heracles, who was said by the Alexander historians (Onesicritus?) to have settled the ancestors of the Sibians in India, because they had been unfit for the onward march (Curtius 9.4.2 & Diodorus 17.96.2).

7) *A temple of unsurpassed magnificence to be dedicated to Athena at Troy*

Strabo 13.1.26 refers to the same project: "It is said that the city of the present Ilians [Trojans] was for a time a mere village, having its temple of Athena, a small and cheap temple, but that when Alexander went up there after his victory at the Granicus River he adorned the temple with votive offerings, gave the village the title of city, and ordered those in charge to improve it with buildings, and that he adjudged it free and exempt from tribute; and that later, after the overthrow of the Persians, he sent down a kindly letter to the place, promising to make a great city of it, and to build a magnificent sanctuary, and to proclaim sacred games."

8) *A tomb for Philip emulating the Great Pyramid (at Giza)*

There is no direct statement of this plan in any other source, but there are circumstantial strands of evidence that make it highly credible. Firstly, Alexander had undoubtedly seen the Giza pyramids, since his route in Egypt passed by them and it would hardly be surprising, if they inspired emulation in him. We also know that the pyre and tomb of Hephaistion seems to have had a stepped pyramidal design. Finally, modern archaeology has revealed that a little while after Alexander's death a very large earth tumulus was indeed heaped over the royal Macedonian tombs at Aegae, one of which probably belonged to Philip.

Thus it would appear that Alexander's ambition to aggrandize Philip's tomb was shared by his successors.

In summary, we find that the great bulk of the material in the Last Plans is echoed elsewhere in the sources. It would also be fair to say that many of these echoes occur in sources that we know to have used Cleitarchus, which is supportive of the view that Diodorus took the Last Plans from Cleitarchus. Insofar as any aspects of the Last Plans are not precisely corroborated elsewhere, they are nevertheless in conformity with what we know of Alexander's policies and motives. I know of no convincing argument against the authenticity of any of the Last Plans.

Antipater & Cassander as Regicides

As has already been argued in discussing the cause of Alexander's death, the theory that Antipater had instigated a poisoning conspiracy holds little water. Indeed, it seems as though Cleitarchus himself had doubts about its credibility and merely cited it for completeness. Antipater seems in fact to have shown some considerable loyalty to Alexander's house above his own, for he conspicuously avoided making his son Cassander his own successor, instead appointing Polyperchon. Subsequent events suggest that he may have acted out of concern for the safety of Alexander's wife and son in Cassander's power. Hence I am inclined to acquit Antipater of the charge of treason.

Conversely, it is hardly even controversial that Cassander became a serial murderer of Macedonian royalty just as suggested by Cleitarchus' closing paragraphs. Firstly, he orchestrated the execution of Olympias, as detailed by Justin 4.6 and Diodorus 19.51.4-5:

As Olympias refused to flee, but on the contrary was ready to be judged before all the Macedonians, Cassander, fearing that the crowd might change its mind if it heard the queen defend herself and was reminded of all the benefits conferred on the entire nation by Alexander and Philip, sent two hundred soldiers who were best fitted for such a task, ordering them to slay her as soon as possible. They, accordingly, broke into the royal house, but when they beheld Olympias, overawed by her exalted rank, they withdrew with their task unfulfilled. But the relatives of her victims, wishing to curry favour with Cassander as well as to avenge their dead, murdered the queen, who uttered no ignoble or womanish plea.

Six years later he perpetrated the murder of Alexander the son of Alexander together with his mother Roxane as related by Diodorus 19.105.2-3:

Now Cassander perceived that Alexander, the son of Roxane, was growing up and that word was being spread throughout Macedonia by certain men that it was fitting to release the boy from custody and give him his father's kingdom; and fearing for himself, he instructed Glaucias, who was in command of the guard over the child, to murder Roxane and the king and conceal their bodies, but to disclose to no one else what had been done.

Not long afterwards he bribed Polyperchon to extinguish the breath of the last of Alexander's sons according to Plutarch, *Moralia*, On Compliancy 530D:

The Reconstruction Of Book 13 Of Cleitarchus

Polyperchon agreed with Cassander for a hundred talents to do away with Heracles, Alexander's son by Barsine, and proceeded to invite him to dinner. When the youth, suspecting and dreading the invitation, alleged an indisposition, Polyperchon called on him and said: "Young man, the first quality of your father you should imitate is his readiness to oblige and attachment to his friends, unless indeed you fear me as a plotter." The youth was shamed into attending; and they gave him his dinner and strangled him.

It is no wonder that Cleitarchus seems to have commented that the sufferings of Cassander and his own sons were a species of divine retribution.

The Itinerant Corpse

The intricate and protracted adventures of Alexander's corpse after his death constitute a story on the same scale as his exploits whilst still alive. I have given full accounts in my earlier books, *The Lost Tomb of Alexander the Great* and *The Quest for the Tomb of Alexander the Great*, to which I must refer the reader desiring more than the outline of how the remains reached Alexandria, which is the limit of my ambition here.

According to my reconstruction, Cleitarchus would appear to have made three important contributions on the matter:

1) In Section 13.45 (below) Cleitarchus states that Alexander had asked on his deathbed that his corpse should be delivered to Ammon in Egypt. Other early sources (notably the *Liber de Morte* in the *Metz Epitome* and Lucian, *Dialogues of the Dead* 13) seem to agree at least that he had requested conveyance of his remains to Egypt.

2) In Section 13.78 Cleitarchus probably incorporated the appointment of Arrhidaeus (not Philip III, but a Macedonian officer) to oversee the preparation of a catafalque and to escort the corpse to Ammon in Egypt among the list of decisions regarding the *First Division of the Satrapies* made at Babylon in June 323BC. Other sources (notably Arrian in the epitome of his *Events after Alexander* made by Photius) agree that Arrhidaeus had been appointed to perform such escort duties, but they differ on the intended destination: in particular, Pausanias 1.6.3 states that the body's objective was Aegae in Macedon.

3) In Section 13.87 Cleitarchus seems to have concluded with a statement of the undoubted truth: that Alexander was initially entombed at Memphis in Egypt, but subsequently transferred to Alexandria, where he lay when Cleitarchus wrote.

It is rather likely that some further information filling the gap between items 2) & 3) has been edited out from Cleitarchus' full version by the intermediaries, but a judicious conflation of numerous fragmentary pieces of information from elsewhere has enabled me to compile the following probable outline of the journey travelled by Alexander's body.

The Death of Alexander the Great by Andrew Chugg

It seems most probable that Cleitarchus was correct in reporting that Alexander's expressed wishes were respected in the impassioned atmosphere of the immediate aftermath of his death. Hence, a plan to send the corpse to Egypt was hatched and Perdiccas appointed Arrhidaeus, perhaps because he was close to Ptolemy, who was appointed to govern Egypt. A splendid catafalque was duly fabricated over a period straddling two Attic years. In the meantime, Perdiccas will have been in communication with Olympias back in Europe. She will have been horrified at the prospect of an Egyptian funeral with mummification and burial instead of a traditional funeral pyre: there is a hint of this in Aelian, *Varia Historia* 13.30, where Olympias groans on hearing that her son had lain unburied for a long period. Perdiccas badly needed her support. Aelian, *Varia Historia* 12.64 tells a story that Aristander of Telmissus gave a prophecy that the land that received Alexander's body would forever remain unconquered. It is tempting to see in this an artifice to persuade the Macedonians that the corpse should be re-directed to Macedon. At any rate, sending it to Aegae became Perdiccas' policy.

The exact date is quite uncertain, but most probably in the Autumn of 322BC the catafalque set forth from Babylon heading NW towards Syria, ostensibly bound for Macedon in accordance with Perdiccas' instructions. Diodorus 18.28 gives a thrilling description of its splendours, which is the basis for the reconstruction shown in Figure 2.7. Some time around the turn of 322BC into 321BC the procession reached northern Syria and suddenly turned southwards towards Damascus, for Ptolemy, who still wished the corpse to be taken to Egypt, had suborned Arrhidaeus. Ptolemy's motive is uncertain, but what evidence there is (Lucian, *Dialogues of the Dead* 13 and the *Alexander Romance* in its Armenian manuscripts) suggests that Ptolemy had made a faithful promise to the dying Alexander to fulfil his wishes in this matter.

Figure 2.7. A reconstruction of Alexander's catafalque (19th century engraving from the author's collection).

Perdiccas was wintering in Pisidia some seven hundred miles away, but couriers brought him word within a week or two. He sent his lieutenants Attalus and Polemon in hot pursuit with a large contingent of cavalry. However, Ptolemy had already met up with Arrhidaeus at Damascus, having come north by arrangement to escort his prize back to his satrapy. The stories in Aelian tell us that Perdiccas' men clashed with Ptolemy's somewhere in Palestine, but that Ptolemy used a decoy hearse to thwart his opponents. It is certain that he was successful in safely conveying Alexander's mummy to Memphis in Egypt, then still its capital.

A wrathful Perdiccas invaded Egypt with the Grand Army in the Spring of 321BC, but he was assassinated by his own men having twice failed to force the crossing of the Nile, whilst sustaining huge casualties through drowning and the marauding of the river's crocodiles. Ptolemy attended a tearful assembly of reconciliation with the survivors, before sending them back north and turning his attentions to the business of Alexander's funeral and entombment.

Various strands of evidence are suggestive of the following scenario for Alexander's first tomb at Memphis. It seems that there existed an empty sarcophagus and a partially complete tomb on the eastern side of the Serapeum temple complex in the Memphite necropolis of North Saqqara, which had been prepared for the last native Egyptian pharaoh, Nectanebo II (or Nakhthorheb). This man had been forced to flee south to Ethiopia in about 341BC to escape a Persian invasion. As far as we know, he never returned, so his intended tomb still lay vacant in 321BC. The empty sarcophagus was found in Alexandria in 1801 by Edward Daniel Clarke and shipped to the British Museum, where it remains on display (Figure 2.8). Clarke recorded that the Alexandrians had asserted that it had once been the sarcophagus of Alexander the Great.

Figure 2.8. The sarcophagus found in Alexandria and made for Nectanebo II: it may have housed Alexander's corpse after it reached Egypt (photo by the author).

This makes sense, if Ptolemy had adapted Nectanebo's empty tomb to serve for Alexander. The hypothesis is corroborated by the fact that Auguste Mariette uncovered a temple with cartouches of Nectanebo II at the eastern end of the Serapeum in 1850-1851. Its main entrance was guarded by a lifesize semicircle of statues of Greek poets and philosophers (see a photo taken during the excavations in Figure 2.9). A side-entrance was guarded by an array of four lions. A windowless chamber unearthed at the end of a side-passage neatly fits the sarcophagus in the British Museum. The statues include several figures of relevance to Alexander's career: especially Homer, Alexander's favourite poet, Pindar, whose house and descendants Alexander protected at Thebes, and Plato, who was the mentor of Aristotle, Alexander's own tutor.

Figure 2.9. The semicircle of Greek philosophers and poets excavated by Mariette in the Serapeum at Saqqara (photo circa 1851).

It is, however, certain that Alexander's tomb was subsequently relocated to Alexandria as reported by Curtius 10.10.20 and therefore incorporated in the penultimate sentence of my reconstruction of Cleitarchus. Several ancient sources (Strabo 17.1.8, Aelian, *Varia Historia* 12.64 & Diodorus 18.28.3) fail even to mention the sojourn at Memphis, notwithstanding the fact that it probably lasted around forty years. But there is a clear indication of the duration of the first entombment at Pausanias 1.7.1, where it is stated that Philadelphus, the son of Ptolemy, transferred the body from Memphis to Alexandria. This cannot have happened before ~290BC, since Philadelphus was not born until 309-8BC. Most probably it happened shortly after his father's death at the beginning of 282BC. Presumably the sarcophagus was transferred with the corpse, thus explaining its presence in Alexandria two thousand years later.

If, therefore, Curtius was still following Cleitarchus at the end of his work, which is the most likely scenario, then Cleitarchus cannot have published his

The Reconstruction Of Book 13 Of Cleitarchus

account of Alexander's career much earlier than 280BC. Furthermore, if we were to seek an historical event, which might have prompted Cleitarchus to publish his volumes *Concerning Alexander*, then we should be looking for something that concerned Alexander in Alexandria around 280BC, which I previously concluded in *Alexander the Great in India* were the most likely place and time for the compilation of Cleitarchus' work. Clearly, the transfer of Alexander's tomb to Alexandria is the outstanding candidate. Hence it is consistent and fitting that the move to Alexandria is the latest and last event in the present reconstruction of Cleitarchus' history.

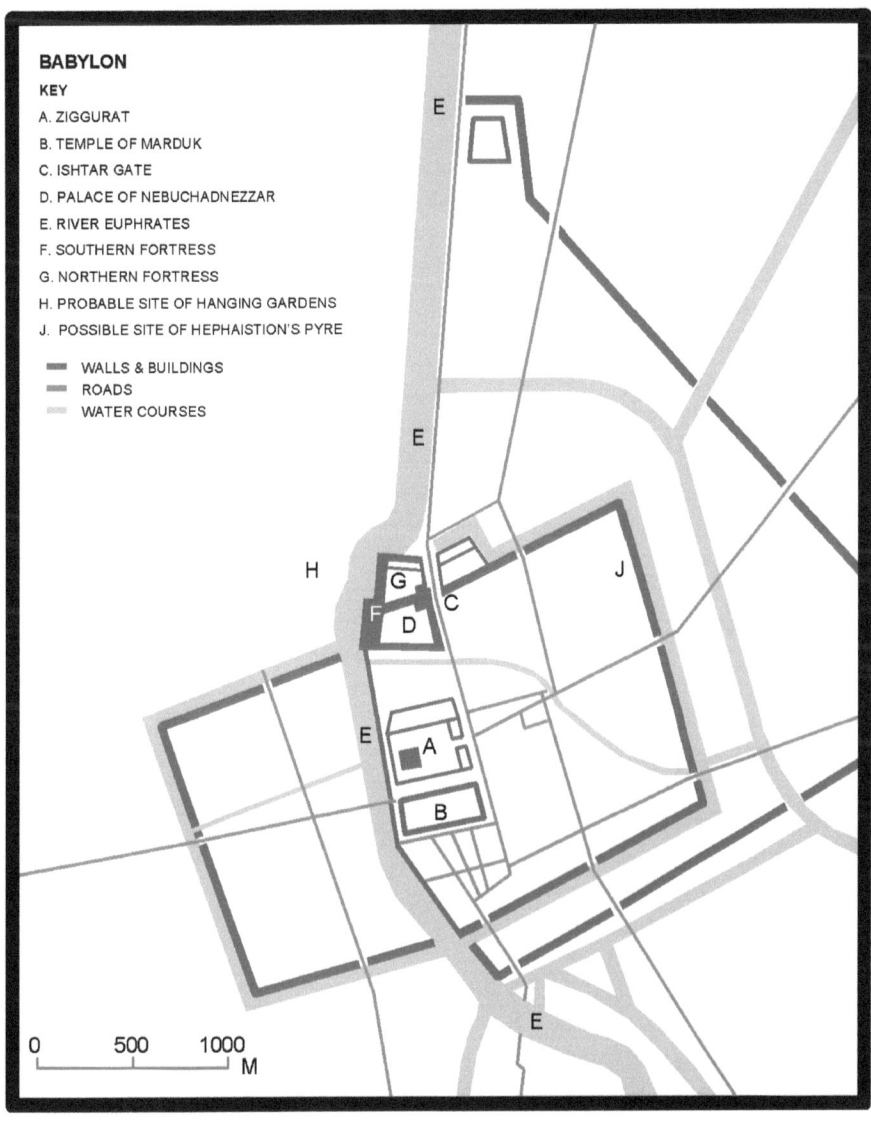

Plan of Babylon according to Robert Koldewey

TABLE 2.1: Close matches between Curtius and Diodorus 17

C=Curtius, D=Diodorus, J=Justin, S=Schwartz, H=Hamilton in Cleitarchus & Diodorus 17, cf.=vergleiche in Schwartz

C3.2.1=D17.30.7 S
C3.11.7-11=D17.34.2-6 S
C3.11.20,23-6=D17.35.2,36.5,2,4 cf.J11.9.11-12 S
C3.11.27=D17.36.6 H
C3.12.15-17=D17.37.5-6 H
C3.12.26=D17.38.2 H
C4.1.15-26=D17.47.1-6 H
C4.1.27-33=D17.48.2-4 S
C4.1.39-40=D17.48.1-2 S
C4.2.7=D17.40.4 S
C4.2.12=D17.41.3-4 S
C4.2.18=D17.40.5 S
C4.2.20=D17.41.1 S
C4.3.6,9,11-12=D17.42.5-6,43.3 S
C4.3.20=D17.41.2 cf.J11.10.14 S
C4.3.22=D17.41.8 H
C4.3.25-26=D17.44.1-3 S
C4.4.1-2=D17.45.7 S
C4.4.3-5=D17.41.5-6 H
C4.4.10-12,17=D17.46.2-4 S
C4.5.11=D17.48.6 S
C4.6.30=D17.49.1 S
C4.7.1,5,9=D17.49.2-4 S
C4.7.12-14=D17.49.4-5 S
C4.7.16-17,20-28=D17.50.3-51.3 S
C4.9.4-5=D17.53.1-2 H
C4.13.26-29=D17.57.1-4 S
C4.15.9-11=D17.59.6-7 S
C4.15.16-17=D17.58.4-5 S
C4.15.28-29,32=D17.60.2-4 S
C4.16.31-32=D17.61.3 S
C5.1.10-11=D17.64.3 S
C5.1.40-42=D17.65.1 S
C5.1.43-45=D17.64.5-6 S
C5.1.25-26=D2.7.3-4 (Jacoby F10) S
C5.1.34-35=D2.10.4,1 S
C5.2.1-7=D17.65.2-4 cf.D17.27.1-2 S
C5.2.8, 12-15=D17.65.5,66.2-7 S
C5.3.1.2,4-5,10=D17.67.1-2,4-5 S
C5.3.17-18,23&C5.4.2-4,10,12,18=D17.68.1-6 S
C5.5.2-4=D17.69.1-2 S
C5.5.5-9,12,23-24=D17.69.2-8 cf.J11.14.11-12 S

The Reconstruction Of Book 13 Of Cleitarchus

C5.6.1-5,8,9=D17.70.1-71.2 S
C6.2.15=D17.75.1 S
C6.4.3-6=D17.75.2 S
C6.4.18,22=D17.75.3,6 S
C6.5.11-12,18-21=D17.76.3-8 S
C6.5.24-26,30-32=D17.77.1-3 cf. J12.3.5-7 & Strabo11.5.4 S
C7.1.5-9=D17.80.2 S
C7.2.18=D17.80.3 S
C7.2.35-37=D17.80.4 cf. J12.5.4-8 S
C7.3.1,3=D17.81.1-2 S
C7.3.5-18=D17.82 S
C7.3.22-23=D17.83.1-2 S
C7.4.33,38=D17.83.4-6 S
C7.5.28-35 cf. Dκ S
C7.10.4-9 cf. Dκβ S
C7.10.15-16 cf. Dκδ S
C8.1.11-19 cf. Dκς S
C8.5.4 cf. Dλα, J12.7.5 S
C8.10.5-6 cf. Dλβ S
C8.11.2=D17.85.1-2, J12.7.12 S
C8.11.3-4=D17.85.4-5 S
C8.11.7-8,25=D17.85.3,8-9&D17.86.1 S
C8.12.1-3=D17.86.2 S
C8.12.4-10,14=D17.86.3-7 S
C8.14.3=D17.87.5 S
C9.1.1,3-4,6=D17.89.3-6&D17.90.1 S
C9.1.8-12=D17.90.4-7 S
C9.1.24-33=D17.91.4-D17.92.3 S
C9.3.10-11=D17.94.2 S
C9.3.19=D17.95.1-2, J12.8.16 S
C9.3.20,23=D17.95.3,5 S
C9.4.1-2,5=D17.96.1-3 S
C9.4.8-14=D17.97.1-3 S
C9.7.16-26=D17.100.2-D17.101.6 S
C9.8.4-8=D17.102.1-4 S
C9.8.13-15(Jacoby F25)=D17.102.6 S
C9.8.17-28=D17.103, J12.10.2-3 cf. Cic. de divin. 2.135 S
C9.10.5-11,17-18,27=D17.104.4-D17.106.1 S
C10.2.4,8-12,30=D17.109.1-2 S
C10.5.21-25=D17.118.3, J13.1.5-6 S
C10.10.14,18-19=D17.117.5&D17.118.2 cf. J12.13.10 S

TABLE 2.2: The First Division of the Satrapies – Vulgate Sources

TERRITORY	DIODORUS 18.3	JUSTIN 13.4.9-25	CURTIUS 10.10.1-4	CLEITARCHUS
"WEST"	-	-	-	-
ARABIA (PART)	-	Ptolemy	-	-
LIBYA/AFRICA	-	Ptolemy	Ptolemy	Ptolemy
EGYPT	Ptolemy	Ptolemy	Ptolemy	Ptolemy
SYRIA	Laomedon	Laomedon	Laomedon	Laomedon
COELE-SYRIA	-	-	-	-
PHOENICIA	-	-	Laomedon	Laomedon
CILICIA	Philotas	Philotas	Philotas	Philotas
GRT. MEDIA	Pithon	Illyrian Pithon	Pithon	Illyrian Pithon
PAPHLAGONIA	Eumenes	Eumenes	Eumenes	Eumenes
CAPPADOCIA	Eumenes	Eumenes	Eumenes	Eumenes
EUXINE COAST	(Eumenes)	-	(Eumenes)	Eumenes
PAMPHYLIA	Antigonus	Nearchus	Antigonus	Antigonus
LYCIA	Antigonus	Nearchus	Antigonus	(deputy Nearchus)
GRT. PHRYGIA	Antigonus	Antigonus	Antigonus	Antigonus
LYCONIA	-	-	-	-
CARIA	Cassander	Cassander	Cassander	Cassander
LYDIA	Meleager	Menander	Menander	Menander
HELL PHRYGIA	Leonnatus	Leonnatus	Leonnatus	Leonnatus
THRACE	Lysimachus	Lysimachus	Lysimachus	Lysimachus
CHERSONESE	-	-	-	-
EUXINE (EURO)	-	Lysimachus	Lysimachus	Lysimachus
MACEDONIA	Antipater	-	-	Antipater
EPIRUS	-	-	-	-
GREECE	-	-	-	-
ILLYRIA	-	-	-	-
INDIAN REALMS	Taxiles & Porus	Taxiles	"retained"	Taxiles & Porus
(CAUCASUS of) PAROPAMISUS	Oxyartes	Oxyartes	-	Oxyartes
INDIA (rest of)	Pithon	Pithon, son of Agenor	-	Pithon, son of Agenor
ARACHOSIA	Sibyrtius	Sibyrtius	-	Sibyrtius
KEDROSIA	Sibyrtius	Sibyrtius	-	Sibyrtius
ARIA	Stasanor	Stasanor	-	Stasanor
DRANGIANA	Stasanor	Stasanor	-	Stasanor
BACTRIA	Philip	Amyntas	"retained"	Philip
SOGDIANA	Philip	"Sulceos Staganos"	"retained"	Philip
PARTHIA	Phrataphernes	Philip	-	Phrataphernes
HYRCANIA	Phrataphernes	Phrataphernes	-	Phrataphernes
PERSIA	Peucestes	Peucestes	-	Peucestes
CARMANIA	Tlepolemus	Tleptolemus	-	Tlepolemus
LESSER MEDIA	Atropates	Atropates	-	Atropates
SUSIANA	-	Coenus	-	Coenus
BABYLONIA	Archon	Archon of Pella	-	Archon of Pella
MESOPOTAMIA	Arcesilaus	Arcesilaus	-	Arcesilaus
ARBELITIS	-	-	-	-
COMPANIONS	Seleucus	~Seleucus	-	Seleucus

The Reconstruction Of Book 13 Of Cleitarchus

TABLE 2.3: The First Division of the Satrapies – Arrian & Others

TERRITORY	ARRIAN 1st F1.5-9 (PHOTIUS)	DEXIPPUS 82.62B (PHOTIUS)	ARRIAN 2nd F9.34-38 (PHOTIUS)	METZ EPITOME 116-122
"WEST"	Ptolemy	-	Ptolemy	-
ARABIA (PART)	(deputy	-	-	-
LIBYA/AFRICA	Cleomenes)	Ptolemy (deputy	Ptolemy	-
EGYPT		Cleomenes)	Ptolemy	Ptolemy
SYRIA	Laomedon	Laomedon	Laomedon	Pithon?
COELE-SYRIA	-	-	-	Meleager
PHOENICIA	-	-	-	Meleager
CILICIA	Philotas	Philotas	Philoxenus	Nicanor
GRT. MEDIA	Pithon	Pithon	Pithon	"Craterus"[29]
PAPHLAGONIA	Eumenes	Eumenes	-	Eumenes
CAPPADOCIA	Eumenes	Eumenes	Nicanor	Eumenes
EUXINE COAST	Eumenes	Eumenes	-	-
PAMPHYLIA	Antigonus	Antigonus	Antigonus	Antigonus
LYCIA	Antigonus	-	Antigonus	Antigonus
GRT. PHRYGIA	Antigonus	Antigonus[30]	Antigonus	Antigonus
LYCONIA	-	-	Antigonus	-
CARIA	Asander	Asander	Asander	Cassander
LYDIA	Menander	Menander	Cleitus	-
HELL. PHRYGIA	Leonnatus	Leonnatus	Arrhidaeus	Leonnatus
THRACE	Lysimachus	Lysimachus	-	-
CHERSONESE	Lysimachus	Lysimachus	-	-
EUXINE (EURO)	Lysimachus	-	-	Antipater to hold everything west of River Halys
MACEDONIA	Antipater & Craterus	Antipater	-	
EPIRUS		-	-	
GREECE		Antipater	-	
ILLYRIA		Antipater	-	Holcias
INDIAN REALMS	-	Taxiles & Porus	Taxiles & Porus	Taxiles & Porus
PAROPAMISUS	-	Oxyartes	Oxyartes	Oxyartes
INDIA (rest of)	-	Pithon	Pithon, son of Agenor	-
ARACHOSIA	-	Sibyrtius	Sibyrtius	Sibyrtius?
KEDROSIA	-	Sibyrtius	-	Sibyrtius?
ARIA	-	Stasanor	Stasander	Stasanor?
DRANGIANA	-	Stasanor	Stasander	Stasanor?
BACTRIA	-	-	Stasanor	Philip
SOGDIANA	-	Philip	Stasanor	-
PARTHIA	-	-	Philip	Pratraphernen
HYRCANIA	-	Radaphernes	-	Pratraphernen
PERSIA	-	Peucestes	Peucestes	Peucestes
CARMANIA	-	Neoptolemus	Tlepolemus	Phtolomeo
LESSER MEDIA	-	-	-	-
SUSIANA	-	Oropius then Coenus	Antigenes	Coenus
BABYLONIA	-	Seleucus	Seleucus	Seleucus
MESOPOTAMIA	-	Archelaus	Amphimachus	-
ARBELITIS	-	-	Amphimachus	-
COMPANIONS	-	-	Cassander	-

---

[29] It is likely that this originally read Pithon Crateuae (Pithon the son of Crateuas).

[30] Photius' summary of Dexippus has: "Cilicia as far as Phrygia".

3. Book 13: July 324BC – July 323BC & Beyond

The Flight of Harpalus; The Exiles Decree; The Mutiny at Opis; Death of Hephaistion; The Cossaeans; Death in Babylon; Aftermath & Entombment

KEY
<u>**Underlined bold text for attributed Fragments of Cleitarchus**</u>
Bold text where there is overwhelming evidence
Bold italic text where there exists direct-firm evidence
Normal text where direct-weak evidence applies
Italic text where the evidence is conjectural
Grey text for connecting passages, if Cleitarchus' version is indeterminate

13.1 *At the outset of the thirteenth and final year of his reign,* ***Alexander received a letter from Coenus***[1] ***recounting events in Europe and Asia*** *Minor,* ***whilst the King had been engaged upon the conquest of India. Zopyrion, Alexander's governor of Thrace*** *and Pontus,* ***had launched an expedition*** *comprising 30,000 men* **against** *the Scythians and had attacked* **the Getae,** *for he reckoned himself a loafer, if he stayed inactive.* ***But sudden gales and tempests had overwhelmed his entire force*** *and engendered its destruction.*[2] *Hence Zopyrion paid the ultimate price for an unprovoked assault upon an inoffensive nation.* **On receiving word of this debacle, Seuthes had compelled the Odrysians, who were his subjects, to revolt. Thrace being all but lost, not even Greece** *was secure.*

13.2 Alexander had entrusted Harpalus with the custody of the treasury in Babylon and of the revenue streams that flowed into it too. Yet once he heard that Alexander had carried his campaigns into India, Harpalus supposed his sovereign to have ventured beyond returning, so he abandoned himself to a life of luxury. Though charged as satrap with the governance of vast territories, he made his priorities the debauching of women and lawless lechery with the foreigners, thereby frittering away

---

[1] Probably either that Coenus who was later governor of Susiana or else Curtius has mistranslated a phrase such as ἀπὸ τοῦ κοινοῦ meaning the government in Macedon.

[2] Cf. Macrobius, *Saturnalia* 1.11.33.

Book 13: July 324BC – July 323BC & Beyond

much of the treasure on wanton pleasure. He had a great freight of fish fetched from as far as the Erythraean Sea and adopted an exorbitant lifestyle, hence making himself the object of widespread criticism.

13.3 Thereafter <u>he engaged Pythionicê</u>, the most celebrated courtesan of her time, shipping her in from Athens. Whilst she lived, he showered her with queenly gifts, <u>and when she died</u> he gave her a fabulous funeral and erected an extravagant monument in the Attic style for her tomb. Afterwards <u>he imported another Athenian courtesan named Glycera and upon her arrival he ensconced her in the palace at Tarsus, where she</u> lay in the lap of luxury at vast expense and <u>received royal dignities[3] from its denizens, who addressed her as their queen. Furthermore, it was decreed that none might honour Harpalus with a crown unless another were likewise accorded to Glycera. At Rhossus[4] he stood her effigy in bronze next to his own and ventured so far as to set up a third statue depicting Alexander beside them.</u>[5] But with a view to the vicissitudes of fortune, Harpalus also lavished favours upon the citizenry of Athens with the object of procuring asylum in adversity.

13.4 When Alexander did in fact return from India and executed numerous satraps, who had been accused of delinquency in the conduct of their duties, Harpalus likewise feared parallel punishment *for his similar indiscretions*. Therefore he garnered five thousand talents *of silver*, engaged six thousand mercenary troops and quit the shores of Asia, setting sail for Attica *with a fleet of thirty ships. Hence they rounded Cape Sounion and determined to head for the port of Athens, but* the citizens would not allow them to dock *in such force*. Therefore Harpalus sent his soldiers to land at Taenarum in Laconia,[6] but, retaining some part of his riches, he himself sought sanctuary with the Athenians.

13.5 *Alexander received word of these matters and was equally enraged by the conduct of Harpalus and* the complicity of *the Athenians. Antipater and Olympias demanded that the renegade should be delivered up to them and Alexander commanded that an armada be made ready, meaning to proceed at once against Athens. But whilst he was covertly fomenting this strategy, he received a letter reporting that* Harpalus, having managed to gain admission to Athens, had won over its demagogues with his money, *notably buying a bout of laryngitis for Demosthenes at*

---

[3] I.e. *proskynesis*.

[4] In Syria.

[5] Jacoby fragment 30 of Cleitarchus = Athenaeus 12.50 or 586CD.

[6] A promontory of the Peloponnesian peninsula due south of Sparta.

the cost of a cup of gold.[7] **But a little later,** *an assembly of the citizens had decreed his departure, so that* **he had been obliged to creep away to rejoin his mercenaries at Taenarum. Thereafter, he had voyaged to Crete with his fleet, where he had perished at the perfidious hands of Thibron, one whom he had counted among his Friends.** *An inventory of Harpalus' treasure was performed at Athens, in consequence of which Demosthenes and others among the orators were convicted of having accepted bribes from Harpalus.*

13.6 *Jubilant at this outcome,* **Alexander** *abandoned his plan to sail over to Europe. However, he* **issued orders that the Greek city-states should accept the return of their own exiles, save for those either charged with sacrilege or having the blood of citizens on their hands. This decree he had proclaimed at Olympia, whilst the Olympic Games were being celebrated.**[8] *Lacking the temerity to spurn Alexander's command, although they deemed him to be beginning to undermine their laws, the Greeks even restored such of their property as remained to those they had condemned to banishment.* The Athenians alone, championing not only their own interests but also the public good, would not suffer such a sewage of humanity, being accustomed to government according to their ancestral laws and traditions, rather than the edicts of a king. Hence they barred the exiles from the bounds of their territory, being willing to endure anything but the former excretions of their own city, that had latterly befouled their places of exile.

13.7 Alexander now convened an Assembly at which he **announced that 10,000 of his older Macedonian veterans were to be released from service and would return to their native land.** *Conversely,* he ordered that 13,000 infantry and 2000 cavalry should be designated for ongoing service in Asia, calculating that the continent could be held by a force of moderate size, since garrisons had been established at many sites and his newly founded cities were packed with colonists, who were strongly motivated to keep matters in order. Yet prior to making his selection of which of them he would retain, he proclaimed that all his troops should make a declaration of their debts. **The king had learnt that many were heavily encumbered by their borrowings** and, despite their debentures having been pledged for their dissipations, **he** had **determined to discharge them of these obligations**, so that they might retain their spoils and their plunder, when they went home. The soldiers suspected an ensnarement, such that the spendthrifts could be threshed from the thrifty, hence they long prevaricated *in providing their accounts*. Being wise to the fact that it was shame rather than insubordination that withheld their

---

[7] Plutarch, *Demosthenes* 25-26, attributes this story to Theopompus, who also seems to be Cleitarchus' source for his information on Pythionicê and Glycera.

[8] Cf. Diodorus 18.8.2-7; Justin 13.5.2-5.

Book 13: July 324BC – July 323BC & Beyond

admissions, **Alexander ordered** tables to be set up throughout the camp and **ten thousand talents to be brought forth.** Then, finally, **they declared their debts** in good faith *and the remarkable beneficence of the king in settling them at his own expense was appreciated by their creditors as much as by themselves, since collection had proven as trying as repayment.* Of so much money, **after but a single day just one hundred and thirty talents were left unspent.** Emphatically, that army, though it conquered so many of the richest realms, nevertheless gleaned more glory than booty from Asia.

13.8 It being known that, despite some being sent home, the rest of them would be retained and it being reckoned that the king planned permanently to vest the seat of his government in Asia,[9] **the troops grew heedless of military discipline** and fell into folly, filling the camp with seditious slander. **When summoned to an Assembly, they heckled the king** and began insistently to petition him for their collective discharge, showing their faces disfigured by scars and their greying heads of hair. *They demanded that he assess their length of service rather than their age, asserting that fairness required that those who had enlisted together should all be released at the same time.* **Undeterred either by the reprimands of their officers or any sense of respect for the king,** with maddened militaristic clashing and clamour **they drowned out Alexander as he sought to speak,** openly asserting that they should not be shifted a single step from that spot save towards their homeland. *And they jeered that he should prosecute his wars alone with his father Ammon, if he disdained his soldiers.* **When at last quiet was restored,** though not so much because their position could be shifted, but rather because they thought that the king had been swayed and they were waiting to see what action he would take, **Alexander addressed them.**

13.9 "What then does this sudden turmoil and such shameless and unrestrained anarchy signify? I dread to say, when you have openly flouted my commands and my crown is tottering, for I evidently lack the prerogative either to address or to acknowledge or to admonish you, or even so much as to look you in the face. Admittedly, I have resolved to send some home and a little later to take others onwards with me, and now I witness as much of an outcry from those headed homewards as from those whom I have decided shall follow my vanguard. Where's the sense in this? - Contrary cases causing common clamour! I should like at least to know whether it is those who are staying or those who are going who are moaning at me?" It might have been believed that they all bellowed their response through a single mouth, so concerted was the answer of the entire Assembly: "We are all of us complaining!"

13.10 "No, by Heracles!" Alexander retorted, "I cannot agree that everyone shares your professed grievance, in which the greater part of the army can have

---

[9] Many of the tetradrachms of Alexander minted at Babylon bear a mu-tau-rho monogram, designating it as the *metropolis* or mother-city; this and Strabo 15.3.9-10 suggest that Alexander intended that it should be his capital.

no part, seeing that I have parted with more men than I plan to retain. Assuredly, there is some underlying ill that turns you all against me. For when else has an entire army deserted from its king? Even serfs do not desert their lords en masse, for even they feel ashamed to abandon masters forsaken by the rest. But in truth I am forgetting how rabid your riotousness was and I am striving to administer cures to incurables. By Heracles! All the high hopes I have conceived in you, I consign to ruin, for I have decided to deal with you not as my soldiers - which you have patently ceased to be - but rather as the worst of whinging workmen! In grasping at the liquid assets that flow around you, you are slipping into madness, oblivious of the lowly status from which you were raised up by my generosity. By Heracles! You deserve to grow old in such penury, since you find it easier to aim for adversity than to follow favourable fortune."

13.11 "Behold! Those who were tributary subjects of Illyria and Persia just a short time ago now disdain Asia and the spoils of all its nations. Those who went about half bare as recently as under Philip, now think purple mantles mean. Their eyes cannot endure the gleam of gold and silver, but they hanker after wooden pots, wicker shields and rust-eaten swords. Such was the lustre of your lifestyle, when I took charge of you together with a national debt of five hundred talents, when all the royal chattels were not worth more than sixty. Such were the foundations for the great deeds thereafter: the basis on which nevertheless – may it not tempt fate to utter it – I established my rule across the greatest part of the world. Are you so disenchanted with Asia, which through the glory of your achievements has set you on a par with deities? You are forsaking your king and scurrying back to Europe, when many of you would not have been able to pay your way, had I not liquidated your loans using riches gleaned from Asia! Neither are you ashamed, whilst parading your gross gluttony for the spoils of the conquered peoples, to wish to return to your wives and offspring, to whom few among you will be able to display the rewards of victory. Others among you have even pawned your arms, in the cause of realising such hopes."

13.12 "Fine soldiers I shall be losing! Servicers of their paramours: for this is the sole pleasure left to them from such rich treasure and in this their outlay is not yet spent! Therefore let the roads lie open to my deserters. Get you gone at once! The Persians and I shall protect your rear as you scamper off and I shall detain none of you. O most ungrateful compatriots, relieve me of the sight of you! Gladly will your parents and children welcome you back, when you turn up without your king! They shall come surging forth to meet deserters and renegades! But, by Heracles, I shall transcend your flight and, wherever I may be, I shall see you suffer for it by favouring and preferring those left with me. Furthermore, you shall soon realise how much an army is worth when it lacks a leader and also what resources are vested in my sole self." Thereupon, *deeming further words ineffectual despite* **having cowed the crowd, an incensed Alexander vaulted from the dais into the midst of the ranks of armed troops. Having**

Book 13: July 324BC – July 323BC & Beyond

noted the most outspoken rebels, he seized them one after another, consigning to the custody of his bodyguards a total of thirteen, *none of them daring to offer any resistance.* Who could credit that *a gathering that had been so mutinous a little while before was now* so *petrified by sudden dread* on witnessing colleagues whose conduct had been no more rebellious than the rest being dragged off to chastisement?[10]

13.13 *Alexander now ordered his Persian attendants to cast the thirteen men he had arrested into the river, whilst still fettered. As he was being led away, one among the condemned men addressed the king:* "For how long shall you impose your will through executions and in foreign fashions too? Your soldiers and fellow citizens led away, alas, by their vanquished opponents and dragged to their doom on untried charges. If you judge that we deserve death, at least exchange the executioners." It was a conciliatory reproach, had Alexander been amenable to the realities, but his anger had turned to madness. Therefore, since those to whom the order had been issued had momentarily hesitated, he reiterated that the bound prisoners were to be plunged into the torrent. Yet not even these sentences moved the troops to mutiny. Instead they came before their regimental officers and the king's Friends squadron by squadron craving that if Alexander judged that any were implicated in the earlier offence then they should be slain. They offered their corpses to appease his anger: let him slaughter them *and be assuaged.*

13.14 Whether out of worship of his title, since people ruled by kings are wont to reverence them among the gods, or else out of personal veneration for Alexander, or perhaps out of habitual faith in such assertive enforcement of his rule, they were thoroughly intimidated. At all events, they gave an extraordinary display of humility and in addition were so **far from being riled by the punishment of their comrades-in-arms, when their executions were confirmed** at dusk*, that **they omitted nothing in manifesting the increased dutifulness and compliancy of each of them.** For upon the following day, when they had been denied access to Alexander, admission being confined to Asiatic troops, they wailed mournfully throughout the entire camp, declaring their desire to perish promptly, if the king should persist in his anger. But **Alexander**, being obdurate in everything he set his mind upon, **ordered that an Assembly of the foreign troops should be convened**, whilst the Macedonians were confined to their camp. **Then, when a great throng of the Persian auxiliaries had gathered together, he** engaged an interpreter and **delivered a speech.**

---

[10] Freinshem inferred a lacuna at this point, whereas it appears to me that the material of Curtius 10.4 belongs here, since it follows the arrests, but precedes the executions.

Figure 13.1. Alexander seizes the leading mutineers (André Castaigne, 1899)

13.15 "When I crossed over from Europe to Asia, it was my hope that I should augment my empire with many renowned nations and mighty men. Neither was I misled in giving credence to their reputations. But to this it may also be added

Book 13: July 324BC – July 323BC & Beyond

that *I behold bold men of unshakeable devotion towards their kings.* I had believed that luxury imbued everything here and that excessive bountifulness had overwhelmed you with pleasures. Yet, by Heracles, such is your resilience in mind and body that you cope equally efficiently with military duties and, whilst being brave men indeed, you cherish loyalty no less than valour. Though indeed I now proclaim this for the first time, it has long been my perception. Therefore *I have both recruited a levy from the younger men among you and also introduced them among my regiments.* You have the same arms and the same outfits, but in obedience and compliance with orders you far excel those others."

13.16 "Hence *I joined myself in marriage to the daughter of the Persian Oxyartes, not scorning to raise offspring with a captive. Then afterwards, when I wished to propagate the shoots of my family tree more broadly, I took to wife the daughter of Darius and encouraged my closest friends by my example to beget children with captives, in order through these sacred unions to erase all division between the victors and the vanquished. And consequently you may consider yourselves my compatriots rather than foreign recruits.* Europe & Asia is now one and the same realm. In assigning Macedonian arms to you, I have made you traditional troops instead of outlandish newcomers and *you are my fellow-citizens as well as my soldiers.* All are acquiring the same outward appearance and *it is neither improper for the Persians to adopt the customs of the Macedonians nor for the Macedonians to emulate Persian practices.* Those who are to live as subjects of the same king should enjoy the same rights."[11]

13.17 "Therefore from now on I propose to divide the duties of my personal bodyguards among you as well as my Macedonians." Thereafter, **Alexander selected a thousand of the Persian youths and assigned them as his lifeguards** *in the palace regiment of the hypaspists, in every sense showing the same trust in them as in his Macedonians.* **And he appointed handpicked Persian commanders and granted them elite ranks** *within the army.* He also incorporated the division of the Persian auxiliaries who had received Macedonian training into his army. **When they saw the king escorted by the Persians,** *whilst they themselves languished in disgrace,* **the Macedonian troops** were much vexed, complaining that the king had transposed their foes to fulfil their own functions. Then they **began to repent their behaviour,** *considering that they had been crazed by jealousy and ill temper.* Thus they went, *unarmed and dressed only in their tunics, to the king's pavilion* **and with tears and wails begged an audience with Alexander,** *beseeching him to chastise them as rude ingrates* **rather than prolong their humiliation.**

---

[11] A long lacuna in Curtius begins here and lasts until the soldiers' tears at the king's deathbed.

13.18 *At first* **Alexander** *would not see them, though he had begun to be mollified. Yet the men would not disperse, but stood for two days and nights before the entrance, blubbering and appealing to him as their lord, until at last on the third day he emerged and seeing them in so abject and distressed a condition he himself wept awhile. Then he reproved them mildly, but afterwards addressed them fondly and* **finally received them back into his favour.** By their conciliatory behaviour they persuaded the king to retire 11,000 of the veterans, whilst generously providing that they should continue to draw active service pay. *And he wrote to Antipater that at all the games and in every theatre they should be wreathed and seated to the fore.* He also discharged Polyperchon, Cleitus the White, Gorgias, Polydamas and Antigenes, who were elderly among *the circle of* his Friends. He appointed Craterus to preside over those whom he had released with orders to govern Macedon in place of Antipater, whom he summoned to join him in the stead of Craterus with a force of fresh recruits.

13.19 Alexander proceeded to induct Persians into the army to make up the shortfall created by the departure of the discharged veterans. At this time Peucestes arrived in camp with a force of 20,000 Persian archers and slingers, whom Alexander implanted in companies among his other troops, and by the innovation of this reform he developed an army melded and attuned to his own ideals.

13.20 There now being sons of the Macedonians born to women taken in the course of his campaigns *and orphaned either by the death or the departure of their fathers*, **the king assessed their precise number and found that they totalled around ten thousand. Therefore he apportioned sufficient funds to finance their upbringing in a manner befitting the freeborn and assigned them to tutors to provide them with an appropriate education.**

13.21 *Afterwards Alexander set forth from Susa with his army, crossed the River Tigris and encamped among the hamlets known as Karai.*[12] *From there he proceeded on through Sittacenê for four days and arrived at the place called Sambana. He tarried there for seven days, then, marching the army onwards, reached the Kelones, as they are called, on the third day. A settlement of Boeotians, who were transplanted during Xerxes' campaign, continues to thrive there through to the present time, still remembering their ancestral customs. They are bilingual, being as fluent as the natives in the local tongue, whilst retaining most of the vocabulary in their Greek and also preserving some Hellenic institutions.*

13.22 *Eventually, after a sojourn comprising a number of days,*[13] *the king resumed his progress, deviating from the highway for the purpose of*

---

[12] It is likely that the mutiny took place at Opis on the River Tigris, but this may not have been mentioned by Cleitarchus; we are now detouring through Babylonia en route to Ecbatana.

[13] It would appear that Cleitarchus specified the duration, but the exact number of days has accidentally been omitted from the manuscripts of Diodorus.

Book 13: July 324BC – July 323BC & Beyond

taking in the sights. **Thereby he came within the bounds of Bagistanê, as that divine district is named, which is forested with fruitful orchards and bounteous in every requisite for an indulgent existence.** *At about this time Hephaistion allocated quarters to Euios the flute player that had been assigned to Eumenes, who therefore went with Mentor to complain to Alexander. In anger Eumenes declared that the route to regard was to discard their arms and to resort to piping and theatricality. At this Alexander thought to reproach Hephaistion, but in conferring with him became annoyed with Eumenes for having questioned the royal authority and prevailed upon him to settle his quarrel with Hephaistion. He also persuaded a reluctant Hephaistion to agree to reconciliation with Eumenes.*

13.23 Thereafter he came to a country capable of nurturing huge herds of horses, *including the royal Nesaean mares as Herodotus tells us,* **where anciently they say a hundred and sixty thousand head were grazed. Yet at the time of Alexander's inspection a mere sixty thousand could be mustered,** *the majority having been rustled by thieves. There too Atropates, the Satrap of Media, made Alexander a present of a hundred Amazon women. They were outfitted like cavalrymen, except that they bore hatchets rather than spears and bucklers instead of shields. Some say that their right breasts were smaller than their left and were bared in battle. Alexander soon sent them away from the army, lest they should be raped by either his Macedonian or barbarian levies. But he first told them to tell their queen that he planned to pay her a visit in order to sire progeny by her.* **After spending thirty days in this region he resumed his march.**

13.24 On the seventh day Alexander arrived at Ecbatana in Media, of which it is said that the circuit of its perimeter measures two hundred and fifty stades.[14] **It is the royal seat for the whole of Media and its vaults are replete with riches. Here he rested his army for some time and held a theatre festival in concert with perpetual drinking parties among his Friends. In the course of this merry-making Alexander's** *dearest* **Friend Hephaistion drank a great deal and fell sick** *with a fever. Glaukos, his physician, being absent at the festivities, he had forsaken his dietary restrictions by consuming a boiled fowl and quaffing a full flagon of wine,* **soon after** *which* **he expired. The king was profoundly grieved,** *for he had greatly cherished Hephaistion, not only on account of his outstanding good looks and boyishness, but also by virtue of his compliancy with Alexander's desires. He mourned immoderately, for straightaway he ordered that the tail and mane of every mount and mule should be shorn and he demolished the battlements of the surrounding citadels. He also crucified the unfortunate physician and for a long while banned the blowing of flutes and the sound of music in the encampment.* **Alexander commanded that the cadaver be conveyed in the care of Perdiccas to Babylon, where he planned to stage a funeral of remarkable magnificence.**

13.25 At this time Greece was gripped by tumult and the hatching of political convulsions, which were the genesis of the Lamian War. *This*

---

[14] About 30 miles!

had come about following Alexander's edict that his satraps should disband their mercenary militias, for, when they complied, many of the discharged troops rampaged throughout all Asia, pillaging to furnish their supplies. After a while they began from every quarter to congregate at Taenarum in Laconia. Thither too came the dregs of the Persian satraps and other leaders together with their funds and their forces, so that they amounted to an assembled army. Eventually, they appointed as their general plenipotentiary Leosthenes the Athenian, a man of supremely radiant spirit and most antagonistic towards Alexander's policies. He conferred covertly with the Council of Athens, who contributed fifty talents towards paying his troops and stocking up on arms sufficient to supply immediate requirements. Aiming for an alliance, he dispatched envoys to the Aetolians, who were ill disposed towards the king and in general he did everything to make ready for war. Having foreseen the magnitude of the forthcoming struggle, Leosthenes applied himself *vigorously* to all these preparations.

13.26 *Making warfare a salve for his sorrow,* **Alexander took a task force against the insubordinate Cossaeans, a stalwart race** *of brigands***, who infested the mountains of Media. They had counted on the cragginess of their country and their fighting prowess in order never to become vassals of a foreign overlord, having held their impregnable heights throughout the period of the Persian principate. Hence at the outset they were too vainglorious to be panicked by the proficiency of the Macedonian troops. Yet the king seized possession of the passages through their purlieus and ravaged the bulk of the Cossaean territory. Alexander was foremost in every fracas, slaying many,** *which he said were sacrifices to the shade of Hephaistion,* **and shackling countless more. Thus the Cossaeans were vanquished everywhere and, being distraught that so many were fettered, they were compelled to save these captives by conceding the subjugation of their nation. Hence they gave themselves up to Alexander and secured peace in exchange for compliance with royal commands. It took the king no more than forty days to reduce this race; then he established exceptional citadels among the crags and stood down his forces.**

13.27 After subduing the Cossaean nation, Alexander marched away with his army and headed for Babylon, progressing at a gentle pace with encampments at frequent intervals so as to rest his forces. *He planned to grant audience to the embassies from Europe and to fête Hephaistion with a fitting funeral,* **but whilst he was still three hundred stades distant from the metropolis, the magi known as Chaldaeans, who have grown greatly esteemed for their astrology by foretelling the future through perpetual star-gazing, put forward the most eminent and learned amongst them. From the configuration of the constellations they had foreseen the forthcoming demise of the king in Babylon, so their envoys were delegated to alert him to his impending peril. They were to exhort Alexander to avoid**

Book 13: July 324BC – July 323BC & Beyond

entering the city and to advise him that he could avert the danger by reconstructing the tomb of Bel, which had been demolished under the Persians, but that he must also relinquish his route and bypass the metropolis.

13.28 *The pre-eminent emissary among the Chaldeans, who was dubbed Belephantes,[15] lacked the verve to address Alexander directly through dread of him, but privately conferred with Nearchus, one of the Friends of the king. He divulged every detail and besought him to relate the matter to the king. Consequently Alexander was apprised of the prophecy of the Chaldeans by Nearchus and the king became ever more concerned and disquieted as he contemplated the skill and repute of these men. Ultimately, he sent most of his Friends on into the city, but altered his own course so as to avoid Babylon and established his camp at a range of two hundred stades* across the Euphrates in the long abandoned city of Borsipa.

13.29 *This behaviour caused widespread wonderment, such that many of the Greeks approached Alexander on the matter, in particular Anaxarchus from among the philosophers. When they discovered its cause, they harangued the king with rationales drawn from philosophy and converted him to the extent that he grew scornful of all the arts of augury and most of all those arts extolled by the Chaldeans.* Their predictions were doubtful and deceitful, for what is ordained by Fate is hidden from humans and what is owed to Nature may not be altered. *It was as though his soul had been savaged and his sages had healed it through discourse, in consequence of which he now made an entry into Babylon with his army. Just as previously,[16] its inhabitants hosted his troops convivially and everyone eagerly embraced loose living and licentious revelry, since the requisite services could be procured in profusion.*

13.30 <u>Nearly every nation of the known world had sent envoys to Alexander</u> *with multifarious missions in mind: some to congratulate the king on his conquests, some by awarding him crowns; others to arrange pacts of amity and alliance; many conveying gorgeous gifts; and also some seeking to refute allegations that had been lodged against them. In addition to the races, cities and dynasts of Asia,* many such from Europe and Libya[17] had also sent embassies. *From the latter came Carthaginians and the Libyan* colonies of the *Phoenicians together with those that live upon the Libyan littoral as far as the Pillars of Heracles.* <u>The European delegations</u> *represented the Greek cities, the Macedonians, the Illyrians and most of those dwelling around the Adriatic Sea. The latter*

---

[15] *Belephantes* is essentially Greek for Mouthpiece of Bel.

[16] I.e. just as at the end of 331BC.

[17] By Libya is meant all of Africa west of the Nile Valley.

<u>incorporated</u> *a few from Italy, amongst whom were* **the Romans.**[18] *Emissaries from Spain, Sardinia, Sicily and* the Thracian tribes swelled the throng and there were even representatives of their neighbours, the Gauls: the first occasion on which that people came to prominence in Hellenic affairs. *Alexander was eager to preside over a congregation that seemed assembled from almost every abode on Earth.*

13.31 *Alexander compiled a list of the delegations and scheduled audiences according to the priority with which he wished to respond. First of all he heard those pursuing sacred missions; secondly, those who came bearing gifts; next those who were disputing borders with their neighbours; fourthly, those suffering internal ructions; and fifth in order, those who wished to air arguments against the restitution of their exiles. He received the Eleians initially, and then successively the Ammonians, the Delphians and the Corinthians ahead of the Epidaurians followed by the others: hearing their petitions in order of eminence of their sanctuaries.*[19] *In every instance he strove earnestly to deliver gratifying responses to the emissaries, letting them leave well pleased insofar as was in his power.*

13.32 *When the emissaries had been excused, Alexander became obsessed with the obsequies of Hephaistion. Such was his fervour for this funeral that it not only eclipsed every earthly precedent, but also denied any scope for posterity to transcend its magnificence. Hephaistion had been most beloved amongst those considered his dearest Friends, so he was surpassingly exalted after his passing away. Whilst he had lived, Alexander had favoured Hephaistion above the rest of his Friends, despite Craterus' rating a rival right to his affections. Hence, for example, when one of the Companions had remarked that Craterus was not inferior to Hephaistion in devotion, Alexander had responded that Craterus was devoted to the king, whereas Hephaistion was devoted to Alexander.*

13.33 *On the occasion of their first visit to the mother of Darius, she had mistakenly performed obeisance towards Hephaistion just as if he were the monarch. Her error having been imparted to her, she had been disconcerted, but the king had said: "Don't worry, mother, for indeed he too is Alexander."* And indeed, it may be agreed that **one should view one's friends' misfortunes as one's own and share one's own good fortune with**

---

[18] Jacoby fragment 31 of Cleitarchus = Pliny NH 3.57; this hints that Cleitarchus wrote after 280BC, when Pyrrhus first made the Romans renowned in the Greek world.

[19] Presumably the Eleians represented the sanctuary of Zeus at Olympia; the Ammonians the oracle of Ammon at Siwa; the Delphians their oracle of Apollo; the Corinthians Poseidon and the Epidaurians Asclepios.

Book 13: July 324BC – July 323BC & Beyond

<u>them. Yet it is improper to mourn</u> *immoderately for* <u>dead friends, but instead the diligent devote their care to the welfare of their</u> *living* <u>household.</u>[20]

13.34 *In general, so much authority and latitude of self-expression was vested in Hephaistion through this relationship that when jealousy made Olympias antagonistic towards him, penning invective and menaces against him in her letters, he responded by writing reprovingly. Thus he closed his own letter: "Let you cease your calumnies against us and forswear fulmination and threats. Even if you persist, we shall pay scant attention. You are well aware that Alexander is more important to us than anything else."*[21]

13.35 *In pursuing preparations for the funeral, the king commanded the surrounding cities to furnish it with finery to the best of their means. He also directed every Asian community diligently to extinguish the flames that the Persians call sacred, pending the finish of the funeral. Such was the custom of the Persians upon the demise of their king, so the masses thought the order an awful augury, whereby they supposed the gods foretold the death of the king himself. There were manifested at this time other supernatural signs alluding to Alexander's end, which we shall relate a little later in the wake of our words concerning the funeral.*

13.36 *Each of the Commanders and the Friends sought to humour the king by commissioning idols of Hephaistion fashioned in ivory, gold and such other materials as men deem marvellous. Meanwhile Alexander assembled engineers together with a multitude of artisans, and then razed the ramparts along a stretch of ten stades. He aggregated the baked bricks and evened out a level space to support the pyre, which he erected on a base a stade square. He divided the place up into thirty chambers, supporting the ceilings upon the trunks of palm trees and employing quadrangular forms to fashion the entire edifice.*[22] *Finally, he applied adornments to every outward facing wall.*

---

[20] Fragment 41 of Cleitarchus = Maximi, Eclogae 6.761A; considered doubtful by Jacoby, but apposite in this context.

[21] Hephaistion seems to be represented as having used the *pluralis majestatis* (the royal we) here.

[22] Since $30=4^2+3^2+2^2+1^2$, this was presumably a four stage step pyramid with 4x4 chambers for its square base, 3x3 chambers for the 2nd stage and so on: the ensuing description of the decoration would be congruent with two bands per step (excepting the topmost), but the lower band in each such pair might easily have been projected outwards so as to give the impression of 7 stages, perhaps matching the Babylonian ziggurat.

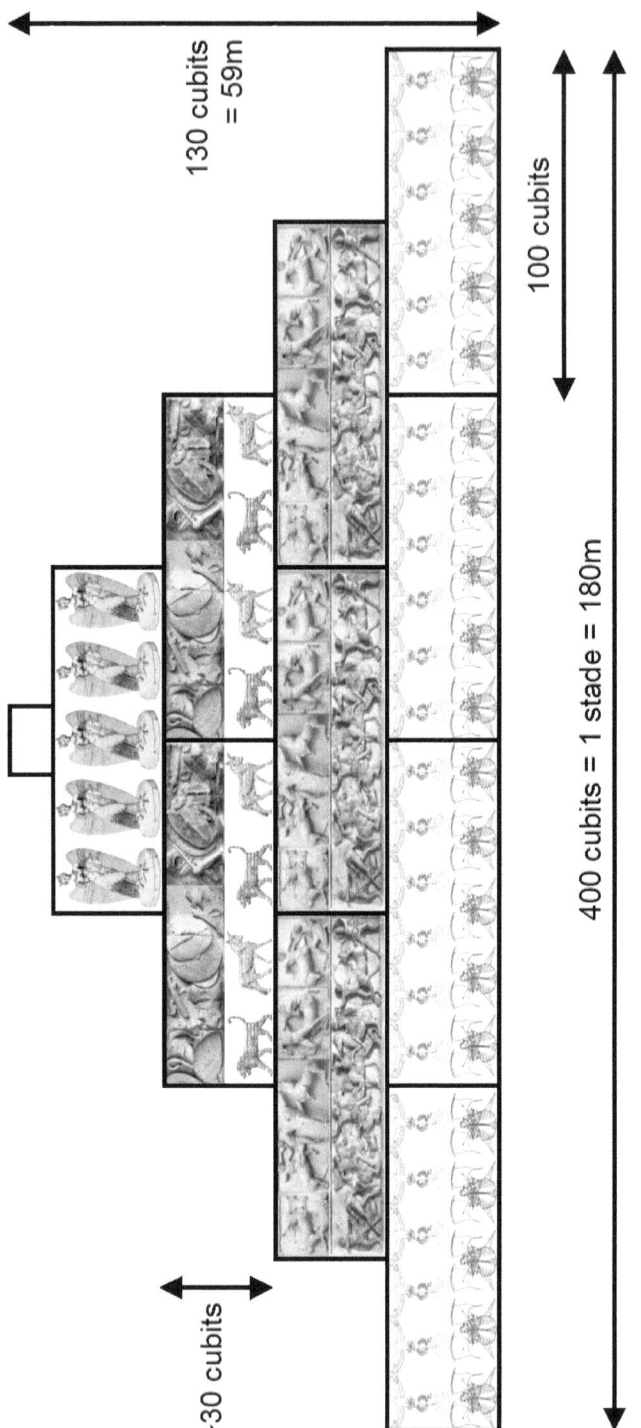

Figure 13.2. A conceptual reconstruction of Hephaistion's Pyre by the author.

13.37 *From around its base there projected the gilded prows of quinquiremes in tight array and totalling two hundred and forty all told. Upon each of their bows there knelt a pair of bowmen, each four cubits high, with effigies of fighting men five cubits tall and red felt flags filling the intervening voids. Above these on the second tier torches towered fifteen cubits in all with golden crowns wreathing their hafts. Wings-spread eagles ascended from the flambeaus, squinting down at serpents that peered up from around the toes. Adorning the third band bevies of beasts were harried by hoards of hunters, whilst in the fourth field was fought a Battle of the Centaurs wrought in gold and for the fifth lions and bulls alternated in bold gilt. The band above was bedecked with both Macedonian and Asian armaments commemorating the courage of the conquerors and the conquest of the conquered. Sirens sitting at the summit had been hollowed to hold hidden humans, who descanted dirges for the departed, and the altitude at the apex of this edifice exceeded a hundred and thirty cubits.*

13.38 *It was universal among the commanders and every class of troops and also the envoys and even the denizens of the district that all strove to compete in embellishing the funeral, hence it is said that the cumulative monetary outlay exceeded twelve thousand talents. As the culmination of these sumptuous obsequies and other distinctions for the deceased, Alexander announced at the finale of the funeral that all should make offerings to Hephaistion as a demigod.*[23] *By chance at this time, Philip of the Friends arrived bearing a pronouncement from Ammon that Hephaistion be hallowed as* half*-divine. Gladdened that the god had endorsed his own estimation, Alexander was foremost in offering sacrifices and he entertained the crowd coruscatingly, for the slaying of all sorts of sacrificial victims entailed a tally of ten thousand.*

13.39 *In the wake of the funeral the king diverted himself in revels and recreation, seeming set at the summit of power and prosperity, yet Fate now sundered the span allotted to his life. Hence Heaven forthwith foretold Alexander's end, as sundry supernatural signs and portents transpired.*

13.40 *Whilst the king was oiled up* for exercising, *so that the royal robes rested with the diadem upon a throne, a shackled detainee from the hinterland slyly slipped his bonds, eluded his guards and passed through the portal of the palace unhindered. He approached the throne, arrayed*

---

[23] The manuscripts of Diodorus had *theos proedros*, but this is corrected to *theos paredros* on the basis of Lucian, *Calumniae non temere credendum* 17, which speaks of sacrifices to Hephaistion as *paredros kai alexikakos theos*; this use of *paredros*, which literally means "one who sits beside", is unusual and in this context seems to mean an assistant god or collaborating deity, which is not greatly inconsistent with the versions of Arrian and Plutarch, which state that Ammon approved honouring of Hephaistion as a hero: the oddity of *paredros* is suggestive of authentic terminology.

himself in the royal raiment, bound the diadem about his brow and set himself upon the seat, where he sat silent and still. The king was alarmed on learning of this illogical lapse, but strode to the throne and concealed his consternation in calmly questioning the fellow as to his identity and his motive in the matter. But he could elicit absolutely no response. Hence the ruler strove to be mild, whilst his subject practiced hauteur, for the diadem does not render its wearer regally wise, but rather it is the mind that makes the monarch and without learning obedience, none should try to rule.[24]

13.41 *Therefore Alexander presented this prodigy to the prophets for prognosis and put the perpetrator to death in conformity with their verdict, hoping that the catastrophe that the culprit's conduct foreshadowed had thereby rebounded upon the man himself. The king retrieved his robes and made offerings to propitiate the gods that ward off wickedness, but his consternation continued unassuaged. He pondered anew the premonition of the Chaldeans and castigated the philosophers that had inveigled him into entering Babylon, for he was bedazzled by the Babylonians' crafts and their clairvoyance, so he commonly cursed those who quibbled in querying the force of Fate.*

13.42 *Shortly thereafter the sacred spirits sent him a second sign regarding his reign. He conceived a yearning to survey the swamps surrounding Babylon, so he set sail in several skiffs with a party of his Friends. His vessel became separated from the rest and strayed by itself during some days, such that he despaired of deliverance. Whilst his boat navigated a narrow channel, where fronds flourished densely and dangled down over the swill, one of them snagged Alexander's diadem and swept it into the swamp. One of the rowers swam to fetch it and, desirous of assuring its safety, laid it upon his own head before swimming back to the boat. After three days and the same number of nights astray Alexander sailed to safety, just as unexpectedly as he had retrieved his diadem, then he again consulted the seers concerning the symbolism of these signs. They exhorted him to perform elaborate sacrifices to the gods and with wholehearted haste.*

13.43 *But the king now resumed his erstwhile custom of convening formal feasts and entirely immersed himself in merry-making for a day and a wakeful night. As at last he was retiring from the revels,* **Medius the Thessalian, one of his Friends, encouraged him to come to a comus** to continue to carouse in company with his companions. **Thereat he downed a great deal of undiluted wine in commemorating the demise of Heracles**[25] **and ultimately sought to drain a brimming,**

---

[24] Fragment 52 of Cleitarchus = Antonii, Melissa 2.1, p.1005C; considered doubtful by Jacoby, but apt in this context.

[25] A festival of the death of Heracles was held annually on Mt Oeta in southern Thessaly.

Book 13: July 324BC – July 323BC & Beyond

gargantuan goblet, but had only gulped half of it, **whereupon he bawled a bellow** *as if he had been skewered* by a spike *piercing his back*. **His Friends lifted and led him away,** for he was in such excruciating pain that he begged for a blade as his remedy and to be touched by anyone was as agonising as a wound. His Friends spread the word that he was suffering from overindulgence in alcohol and *his attendants put him straight to bed and tended him attentively, but his sickness worsened and the medics were mustered. None was able to do anything to aid him, so he endured awful agony and anguish.*

13.44 By the fourth day Alexander sensed his certain death upon him *and he adduced that he detected the doom of his dynasty in it, for the Aeacidae were mostly deceased by their thirtieth year.* **Then the troops were in a ferment**, surmising that their prince was perishing through perfidy; **but Alexander** himself assuaged them all, when, laid out in the loftiest location in the city, he **allowed them all to look upon him. Weeping welled up as they beheld him** proffering his right hand for their kisses. **As their tears burst forth, they appeared not as an army visiting its king, but one attending his funeral. And greater grief gripped those prominent at his bedside.** Yet **Alexander** did not weep but **surveyed them and** asked: "After my passing, how shall you come by a king worthy of such men?" *All were mute, yet he gave no hint of depression, but rather consoled some who could not contain their sorrow and gave others instructions for their parents. His spirit was as invincible in the face of death as it had been in confronting the enemy.* **As incredible to say as to hear, he persisted with that posture, into which he had settled himself ere admitting the military, until he had taken a last salute from the entire army. He then dismissed the lower orders and, as though freed from all life's cares, flung back his limbs in languor.**

13.45 *He bade his Friends draw nigh, since* *after six days* even his voice was now vanishing, and *despairing of living* he *then* removed his ring from his finger and ceded it to Perdiccas. He also issued instructions that they should command that his corpse be conveyed to Ammon. And when his Friends asked him, "To whom do you bequeath your realm?" he responded, "To the strongest." But he added that he foresaw that his foremost Friends would stage famous funeral contests *in his honour.* **Then again, when Perdiccas inquired when he wished divine honours paid to him, he said he wished for them when they themselves were happy. These were the last words of the king,** *for Alexander expired shortly afterwards, having reigned for twelve years and seven months.* His feats were the finest, not just judging by earlier reigns, but also looking at later leaders down to our day.

Figure 13.3. The death of Alexander (1696)

13.46 Initially, the entire palace resounded with woeful wailing, loud lamentation and plaintive plangency. But soon enough, all were numbed by mute melancholy as if in a desolate waste, when in dejection they turned to pondering

Book 13: July 324BC – July 323BC & Beyond

what might now transpire. The noble youths who customarily cared for his person could neither restrain their gargantuan grief nor keep within the courtyard of the royal quarters. Roving around in semblance of fury, they saturated the city in sorrow despite its immense extent, omitting no moaning that mourning mouths in such a dire disaster. Accordingly, those who had stood vigil outside the palace, Macedonians and foreigners alike, swarmed together. And neither could the victors and the vanquished be differentiated in their shared distress, for the Persians commemorated the mildest and most just of lords, whilst the Macedonians bewailed the best and bravest of monarchs, such that between them they staged a kind of contest in grieving.

13.47 Not merely mutters of mourning, but also voices of vexation could clearly be heard to complain that it was the jealousy of the gods that had hauled from the human sphere such a forceful fellow in the flower of his youth and fair fortune. His vigour and his visage as he led his troops into battle, besieged cities, scaled ramparts and at assemblies presented prizes to the valiant were as a vision before their eyes. Then the Macedonians repented having refused him divine honours, confessing their disloyalty and ingratitude in swindling his ears out of an epithet they should have enjoyed. And after lingering long between revering their king and pining at his passing, they turned their pity upon themselves. It was their perception that they had been marched forth from Macedon and forsaken beyond the Euphrates amidst enemies not yet reconciled to their recent rule. Lacking a legitimate heir for their monarch and in the absence of a sure successor to his sovereignty, every contender would be trying to draw the resources of the state to himself.

13.48 Thence they conceived a foreboding of the civil conflicts that were to come. Once more their blood would spurt forth as fresh wounds rent old scars, not now for the rule of Asia, but rather in disputing their own leadership. Decrepit and debilitated, those who had recently requested release from a rightful ruler would perchance perish to preserve the power of some piddling pretender. As they mulled this over in their minds, dusk descended to darken their disquiet. The soldiers stood at arms, whilst the Babylonians peered forth, some from the walls and others from their rooftops, as if they might thus perceive a resolution. Yet none dared set their lanterns alight, so their vision was veiled, but their ears caught the calling and the clamour. Being often possessed by pointless panic, they collided in careering down dark alleys and were mutually shaken and suspicious in such encounters.

13.49 The Persians sheared their shocks and locks in accordance with their custom and got themselves garbed for grieving with their wives and offspring, for they mourned their monarch not as their vanquisher and former foe, but rather with real regret as a most righteous ruler of their own nation. Though accustomed to abiding under kings, they conceded that none other had more deserved to command them. And the lamentation was not confined within the walls of the city, since such terrible tidings had irrupted into the region round about and thence percolated through a prodigious part of Asia on the near side of the Euphrates.

13.50 *Word rapidly reached* the mother of Darius too, *who* was dolorous over Alexander's demise. *Therefore she ripped away her raiment, replacing it with garments for grieving, tearing her tresses and flinging herself to the floor. Settled with her was the second of her granddaughters, but lately bereaved of Hephaistion, whom having married she now mourned, so that the communal despondency accentuated her personal pain. But solely Sisygambis herself suffered for the injuries to her entire kindred: she wept in turn for the ills that had befallen her and her granddaughters. And these fresh frets evoked the pining of the past. You might have thought the woebegone woman had just lost Darius and was about to conduct the last rites for two of her own sons:* she wept for both the dead and the living. Who now would be the guardian of her girls? Who would be the Alexander of tomorrow? They were prisoners once more and robbed of their royal rank all over again. After Darius had died, they had discovered a defender, but in the aftermath of Alexander it was clear that none could be found to care for them.

13.51 *In this context she was conscious that her eighty brothers had been slain in a single day by that most savage sovereign, Ochus, and that the felling of their father had augmented the massacre of so many sons. Of the offspring that she herself had borne, but a single one of seven survived.*[26] *Darius himself had prospered for a little while, merely that he could meet with a more pitiless passing.* So, ultimately, Sisygambis succumbed to sorrow. *Veiling her head* and *turning away from her granddaughter and grandson, who sank down in supplication at her knees,* she spurned *both* sustenance *and* sunlight *and* she was deceased five days after determining to die. *Assuredly* her death is *tremendous testimony for the tenderness of Alexander towards her and for his virtuous treatment of all those taken in his wars:* for she, who allowed herself to live beyond Darius, was ashamed to outlive Alexander.

13.52 And, by Heracles, it is evident to those who evaluate the king evenly that his excellence was innate, whilst his errors were the fault of fate or else immaturity. He exhibited an astounding strength of spirit and nearly inimical tolerance of toil. His bravery was not merely remarkable among rulers, but exemplary even among individuals in whom valour is a singular virtue. Often his generosity rendered richer rewards than are implored from the immortals. His lenity towards the losers led him to release many realms into their rule, either kingdoms captured from them in conflict or else given as gifts. He always disdained the dread of death that paralyses other people. His yearning for praise

---

[26] Oxathres.

Book 13: July 324BC – July 323BC & Beyond

and glory was more than was modest, but was excused by his youth and such superlative deeds. Then there was his devotion towards his parents, of whom he had determined to designate Olympias as a deity and had avenged Philip. Then again there was his beneficence towards almost all of his friends and his benevolence towards his troops. As prudent as he was courageous; wily well beyond the wisdom of his years; self-controlled in his crude cravings and indulging love's longings within limits set by nature, he sampled no sensual pleasures save such as were licit. Indeed these endowments were his natural disposition.

13.53 In consequence of his career prospering, he put himself on a par with the Pantheon and aspired to divine honours, being credulous of corresponding oracular advice. And he was more maddened than was meet by those who refused him reverence. He adopted foreign dress, thus copying the customs of the conquered countries that he had despised before defeating them. As for his irascibility and his lust for wine, seeing as they were exacerbated by his youth, more maturity might have moderated them. Yet it ought to be owned that, though he owed much to his virtue, he owed yet more to Fortune, over whom he alone among mortals held sway. How often she redeemed him from the threshold of Hades! How often, when daring drove him into danger, she guarded him with guaranteed good luck! She also ordained the same end for his life and his glory. The Fates deferred his demise whilst he overwhelmed the Orient and accessed the Ocean, fulfilling every feat that a mortal can manage.

13.54 Such was the sovereign and seignior for whom a successor was sought; yet the burden proved too great to set upon the shoulders of a single soul. So it was that his mere name and the fame of his feats raised rulers and realms across virtually the whole world. And those who kept control of even the slightest slice of his huge heritage were reckoned most renowned.

13.55 But back in Babylon, *whence indeed the discourse has digressed*, **the king's Bodyguards summoned his senior Friends and the commanders of his contingents to** *a parley at* **the palace.** There followed in their footsteps a mob of the military, desirous of discovering who would inherit Alexander's heritage. Quite a few commanders could not reach the royal quarters, being blocked by the teeming troops, despite a declaration debarring any not convened by name from a herald: for, being unwarrantable, his authority was spurned. Initially a sonorous sobbing and sighing resounded anew, but soon silence descended upon them and they tempered their tears as they wondered about what was to come. At this point Perdiccas put in public view the throne, upon which rested the raiment and the diadem of Alexander together with his arms, and he took the ring which had yesterday been yielded to him by the king and set it on the same seat. At such a sight the Assembly once more burst into bawling and fresh gales of grief.

13.56 *And Perdiccas declared:* "I hereby return to you that ring with which the king customarily endorsed edicts concerning his kingdom and his commands, which he himself consigned to my keeping. And, although even the gods in fury could not contrive a calamity comparable with that which has afflicted us, yet, considering the cardinal accomplishments of the king, it is conceivable that such a famous fellow was transfigured by divine will to work in the world of men until his destiny was done and thereupon rapidly reverted to his immortal roots. Therefore, since naught endures of him save what is always sloughed off by immortality, it is firstly fitting that we should perform the rites due to his corpse and his name, being mindful of what municipality and which men we are among and of what kind of president and prince we are deprived! We must manage the matter, my fellow fighters, and consider how we can keep our conquests in the midst of the men we have mastered. We require rulership: whether by one or several is your prerogative. But it is incumbent upon you to realise that a swarm of soldiers without a leader is a body without a soul. **Roxane has been pregnant since** six **months ago. It would be for the best if she should bear a boy, who shall reign over us by the grace of the gods when he comes of age.** Let you lay down by whom you would like to be led in the interim." So spoke Perdiccas.

13.57 Then Nearchus responded that none could wonder than only the blood-kin and lineage of Alexander were well matched to the majesty of the monarchy. However, **to hold out for a king as yet unborn and to overlook him that already existed suited neither the circumstances nor the mood of the Macedonians, for there was a son of the king by Barsine**, namely Heracles at Pergamon, who ought to be endowed with the diadem.[27] This peroration pleased nobody. In accordance with their custom they continually clashed their spears upon their shields in agitation and they were almost moved to mutiny, when Nearchus proved dogged in his dogma. At this point Ptolemy intervened: "*Despite that Alexander did not decree it as he died, it is claimed that* either **Roxane's** or Barsine's **son** is such a suitable successor to rule the race of Macedon! **Being the better part spawned from the spoils, even to speak his name will be an** unholy **shame for Europe. Is this why we have prevailed over the Persians: so that we can pander to their progeny?** Their rightful rulers, Darius and Xerxes, endeavoured ineffectually to accomplish this end with endless thousands of troops and immense armadas. Here's my opinion: the throne of Alexander should be placed in the palace and those he used to call upon to counsel him should convene there whenever communal concerns demand due deliberation. Whatever action the majority move should be mandated and the commanders and captains of the contingents should comply with their will."

13.58 Some sided with Ptolemy, whilst fewer favoured Perdiccas; at which juncture Aristonous began to address them: "When Alexander was asked to whom he relinquished his realm, he desired the designation of the mightiest

---

[27] Justin 13.2.6-7 attributes the remarks about Heracles to Meleager, but it is easy to see that Trogus might have summarised to "Meleager and others", hence Justin's further epitomisation; Nearchus married a daughter of Barsine at Susa in 324BC, so he was Heracles' brother-in-law.

man. Furthermore, he himself appraised Perdiccas as the finest fellow by surrendering his ring into his hands. For he was not the only one who was sat nearby as the king lay dying, but rather Alexander chose him to whom he would hand it by casting his gaze around the throng of his Friends. Therefore it pleased him to place Perdiccas at the pinnacle of power." None doubted that his view was true. Now all called upon Perdiccas to come to the fore and retrieve the ring of the king. But he was in a quandary between desire and dishonour and reckoned the more reluctantly he clutched at that which he craved, the more insistently they would define it as his duty. After hesitating in indecision over how to proceed, in the end he drew back and moved to stand behind those gathered around the throne.

13.59 But Meleager, one of the commanders *who had been sent to suppress the furore amongst the phalanx*, his spirit inspired and spurred by the prevarication of Perdiccas, now proclaimed: "May the gods forefend that Alexander's heritage and the rank of running such a remarkable realm should be shoved upon such shoulders. Certainly, people will not permit it. I speak not of those better born than this fellow, but of blokes such as need not long endure any outcome against their will. In truth it does not matter, whether you recognise as ruler Roxane's son, whenever he be born, or Perdiccas, since that man will seize sovereignty even in the guise of a guardian. That is why he does not wish to accept any king, except one as yet unborn. In the context of our mutual haste, which is not just justified but even essential, he alone would defer the matter for months and already divines that it is a boy that has been conceived. Which of you could doubt that he would even be prepared to provide an impostor? By the god of my faith, if Alexander had left us this man as our monarch in his stead, then this alone of all that he ordered ought not in my opinion to be enacted. Therefore, why should you not rush to raid the treasury? For certainly his citizens are the apparent heirs to the wealth of the king." This speech being spoken, he barged through the midst of the men-at-arms and those who ceded him passage as he departed proceeded to pursue him to the promised plunder.

13.60 So now there was a thick throng of armed troops gathered around Meleager, and the convention veered toward dissension and discord, whereupon a man of the merest rank, not known to very many of the Macedonians, inquired: "Why should there be any work for weapons in civil strife, when **you have the sovereign whom you seek**? There is in the camp **Arrhidaeus, son of Philip and brother to Alexander** that was king just a little while ago and lately his collaborator in ceremonies and sacrifices, and now his only heir, yet overlooked by you. What has he done to deserve this? What deed did he do that he is robbed of rights recognised by all realms? If it's that you seek a second Alexander, you shall never know such again. Else if you wish for one of his kin, there exists only Arrhidaeus." Having heard this, the whole host was hushed at first, as if under orders, but then they clamoured in concert for Arrhidaeus to be called, yelling that those who had convened the conference without him deserved death.

13.61 Then ***Pithon**[28]* in torrents of tears started by saying how Alexander was most to be commiserated on having been defrauded of the friendship and fellowship of such superb citizens and soldiers: for they were so single-minded in their surveillance of the laurels and legacy of the king that all else was veiled from their view. And he **was not at all ambiguous in speaking against the man to whom the realm was being rendered**: *"It is not just on account of his disreputable dam, for he was born of a bawd from Larissa,[29] but also because of the intense imbecility that afflicts him, and lest, were he king in name, some other should wield the authority."*[30] Through throwing in their faces such vehement vitriol, he stirred up more antagonism towards himself than disdain for Arrhidaeus. For their sense of sympathy began to sow their support. Hence with relentless roaring they insisted that they should suffer no sovereign save such as had been sired into the succession and thus they bade that Arrhidaeus be summoned. Meleager promptly propelled him into the palace out of hostility and hatred towards Perdiccas and so **the soldiers saluted him as their sovereign under the pseudonym of Philip** *after his father*.

13.62 Such was the cry of the crowd, but **the foremost fellows** felt differently. Among these Pithon **began to pursue the policy of Perdiccas by proposing Perdiccas and Leonnatus**, **_both related to the royal line_**, as guardians for any future son of Roxane; adding that Craterus and Antipater should be assigned the administration of affairs in Europe. Then an oath *of obedience* was exacted from each of them that they should acknowledge any king begotten by Alexander.

13.63 Not without just cause, Meleager was worried he would be punished; hence he had withdrawn with his faction. But now he burst back into the palace dragging Philip along with him, proclaiming that he was of tempered maturity well suited to the public duties of a new monarch as they had envisaged just a little while ago. Let them merely audition this scion of Philip, son and brother to a brace of kings: let them favour their own feelings foremost.

13.64 Neither oceanic depths nor vast, storm-swept sounds can summon such surges as are seen in the emotions of a mob, especially if it is revelling in a recent yet transient autonomy. Few favoured the freshly picked Perdiccas, whereas many were minded to make their master Philip, whom they had

---

[28] Or possibly Ptolemy: manuscripts of Curtius had *phiton*, but Justin has *ptolomeus* object to Arrhidaeus.

[29] Arrhidaeus was the son of Philip and Philinna, a "dancing-girl" from Larissa, but he seems to have been formally acknowledged by Philip, perhaps in the context of the Pixodarus affair.

[30] The actual words of the denunciation of Arrhidaeus are missing in the surviving text of Curtius, which shows signs of corruption at this point, but a partial reconstruction may be read in from Justin 13.2.11; it is a reasonable hypothesis that Curtius omitted the invective, because he was drawing a parallel between the accession of Arrhidaeus and that of his own emperor, Claudius; cf. Curtius 10.9.3-6.

Book 13: July 324BC – July 323BC & Beyond

disdained. But they were incapable either of opposing or approving anything for long, at some points repenting their plans, at others repenting their repentance. But in the final analysis their affiliation inclined towards the royal line. Arrhidaeus had quit the Assembly having been mightily alarmed by the lordliness of the leading men, yet the effect of his departure was more to muffle rather than diminish his support among the troops. And upon being now recalled, he wrapped himself in the raiment of his brother, the self-same suit as had been set upon the throne. Meleager donned a cuirass and clutched his arms to act as escort to the new king. The phalanx followed suit, smiting their shields with their spears to signal that they would spill the blood of any who aspired to the throne without warrant. They rejoiced that the imperial power would remain with the same house and family. The royal dynasty would duly appropriate their heritage of empire. They were accustomed to respecting and reverencing the name itself and none assumed it save such as were born to reign.

13.65 Therefore in consternation Perdiccas commanded that the chamber in which the corpse of Alexander lay should be bolted. With him were six hundred supporters of proven prowess. And also Ptolemy and the retinue of Royal Pages had coupled themselves to his cause. But the barriers were readily ruptured by so many thousands of men-at-arms. The king too burst in, beset by a cortège of collaborators, among whom Meleager was pre-eminent *with Attalus acting as his accomplice*. Perdiccas, in a rage, rallied any who wished to ward the body of Alexander, but those who had forced their way in flung their javelins at him from afar. And many were wounded, when eventually the veterans doffed their helms, the better to be known, and began to beseech those who were with Perdiccas to refrain from fighting and to defer to the king and force of numbers. Perdiccas was the first to sheathe his arms and the rest followed suit. Then, when Meleager confided that they should not forsake the corpse of Alexander, they supposed he sought to snare them there, so they stole away, passing through part of the palace facing the Euphrates. **The cavalry,** which was constituted from the best-born youths, **fully followed Perdiccas and Leonnatus and favoured faring forth from the city and fighting from the fields.** But Perdiccas did not despair of the foot following him as well. Hence, so it should not seem that he had severed himself from the rest of the army by withdrawing with the cavalry, he stayed within the city.

13.66 Moreover Meleager repeatedly reproached his ruler, saying that his right to reign would best be ratified, if Perdiccas were to perish, since, if his unbridled spirit were not crushed, he would subvert the situation; for Perdiccas knew full well what treatment he deserved from the king and no one was fully faithful to one whom he feared. The king rather heard him out than concurred; and so **Meleager** simply supposed his silence to constitute a command and **arranged** *for Attalus* **to send henchmen to arraign Perdiccas** in the king's name. **They were commissioned to kill him**, if he were to demur. When the approach of these henchmen was heralded, **Perdiccas posted himself** in the entrance to his residence **attended by** a total of sixteen of the retinue of **Royal Pages.** From there he castigated those who came for him, calling them Meleager's minions, and *inviting them to take him on*, but **the determination** of his demeanour and countenance **so cowed them that they fled in consternation**. Thereupon Perdiccas directed the Pages to mount their steeds and got through to Leonnatus with a few of his friends, so as to stage a sturdier stand against any force of foes that might be brought to bear.

13.67 On the following day the Macedonians deemed it a damnable deed that had put Perdiccas in peril of perishing, so they decided to set out in arms to retaliate for the recklessness of Meleager. But he, having foreseen such an insurrection, when he came before the king commenced to coax him as to whether he had not himself commanded the capture of Perdiccas? The king conceded that he had instructed it at the instigation of Meleager, but there was no cause for commotion, since Perdiccas still lived! Therefore, when the gathering had been dispersed, Meleager was panic-stricken in perplexity, particularly due to the defection of the cavalry, for the peril he had previously projected at his opponent had now recoiled upon his own person. He squandered three days as he pondered improbable plans.

13.68 Yet actually even the palace preserved a semblance of its former functioning, for envoys of state still came before the king and the commanders of the forces still stood about him and the antechamber was still stuffed with stewards and armed guards. But the atmosphere of deep despondency was an indication of their dire predicament, and through mutual distrust they did not dare draw together nor discuss matters amongst themselves. Rather they mulled over in their minds their private presumptions and through comparison with the new king they nourished their nostalgia for him whom they had lost. Thus they longed for him whose leadership and guidance they had *formerly* followed, for they were forsaken amidst perilous, unpacified peoples, who would risk retaliating for their many injuries whenever they were availed of an opportunity. Such cogitation was corroding their morale when it was proclaimed that the cavalry commanded by Perdiccas, having seized the countryside surrounding Babylon, had begun to detain the grain being moved into the metropolis. Therefore, firstly frugality then famine set in and those within the city supposed that they had either to reach for reconciliation with Perdiccas or else to resolve the wrangle with their weapons.

13.69 Unintentionally, it so happened that the folk in the farmland, fearing that their villas and villages would be laid waste, were seeking sanctuary in the city, whilst the failure of their food supply moved the townsmen to migrate from the metropolis: to each community the abode of the other seemed safer. Having misgivings of mutiny amongst these migrants the Macedonians met in the palace and gave vent to their views. It was accepted amongst them that they should despatch a delegation to the cavalry to curtail the discord and discuss the discarding of arms. Therefore the king so commissioned Pasas of Thessaly and Amissus of Megalopolis and Perilaus. When they had conveyed the monarch's message, they returned with the response that the cavalry would not set aside their arms unless the king surrendered the sowers of dissension.

13.70 This being promulgated, the soldiers impulsively seized their weapons and the ruction roused Philip forth from the royal quarters, declaring: "There's no use raising a rumpus, for those who rest in repose shall reap the riches of those who vie amongst themselves. Furthermore, be mindful that this is a matter of dealing with compatriots and hastily to hew away their hope of appeasement is to hurtle into civil war. Let us investigate whether they can be assuaged by a second delegation. As the corpse of the king has not yet been buried, I believe all will be allied in discharging this duty to him. As far as I am concerned, I would rather surrender my sovereignty than dispose it through spilling the blood of citizens. So, if there be no other hope of harmony, I beg and beseech you to pick a better man."

13.71 Then with welling tears he took the diadem from his head with his right hand and proffered it, so he who professed to be a fitter fellow might relieve him of it. Such a sober speech inspired high hopes for his character, which had hitherto been bedimmed by the brilliance of his brother. Therefore all present began to prompt him to proceed as he had proposed. Hence he sent back the selfsame emissaries to solicit that Meleager be recognised as a third leader. This was conceded without difficulty, for Perdiccas also desired to distance Meleager from the monarch and he calculated that one would prove unequal to two. Therefore, when Meleager came forth at the fore of the phalanx to meet with him, Perdiccas received him at the head of his cavalry contingents. And each formation hailed the other, united in perpetual peace and staunch solidarity, or so they supposed.

13.72 *But now the Fates were forcing fratricidal conflict upon the Macedonian people, for monarchy brooks no rivals, yet was coveted by many. Hence at first they clashed their men together, then they scattered them about. And when they had burdened the body with more than it could bear, its peripheral parts began to break away and an empire that could have stood sound under a single sovereign was wrecked through being run by sundry rulers.*

13.73 Perdiccas vested his sole hope of salvation in the demise of Meleager, believing his brashness, faithlessness and readiness to revolt as well as his most malign enmity motivated a pre-emptive move against him. But he diligently disguised his designs, the better to catch Meleager unawares. Hence he privately persuaded some from among the forces over which he presided publicly to bemoan the parity of Meleager with himself, as if Perdiccas himself were innocent of their complaints. When Meleager was informed of their invective, in a fuming fury he related what he had learnt to Perdiccas, who, as if horrified by an unheard of happening, began to seem surprised and to groan and to show some semblance of sorrow. In the end, they agreed that they ought to arrest the authors of such seditious prattle. Meleager was moved to thank Perdiccas and to enfold him in his arms, blessing his good faith and goodwill towards him. Then they took counsel together and plotted a plan to crush the culprits.

13.74 *They were pleased to perform a purification of the army* according to the custom of their country and the preceding dissension seemed to provide a plausible pretext for it. The Macedonian monarchs customarily lustrate their troops in the following fashion: they rend a bitch asunder and deposit a part of its flesh on either side at the far end of the field into which they parade the army.[31] All the soldiers stand within this land: hither the horse and thither the phalanx. Accordingly, *on the day* set aside for this sacred rite, the king accompanied by *the cavalry* and the elephants *arrayed themselves facing the foot* commanded by Meleager. As the cavalry contingents came on at them, the foot felt a frisson of fear and anticipation in view of the recent rift, not wholly healed, and they dithered awhile as to whether they should withdraw into the city, since the field favoured the cavalry. Yet reckoning they ought not rashly to refute the good faith of their fellow fighters, they stood their ground, readying their resolution to repulse any assault upon them.

13.75 Now the columns were converging and just a small space separated their foremost files. At this juncture the king commenced to canter up to the infantry with a single squadron of cavalry. Prompted by **Perdiccas** he *insisted that the instigators of the discord,* whom he was actually obligated to protect, *should be given up for punishment,* threatening that he would charge them with all his regiments and the elephants to boot should they refuse. The infantry were stunned by this unforeseen aggression and neither could Meleager himself contribute either counsel or courage to their cause. It seemed for the moment safest to await what might transpire rather than push their luck. Then, perceiving that they were paralysed and punishable, Perdiccas segregated thirty[32] men, who had followed Meleager in sallying forth from the Assembly held just after Alexander's death, and in the sight of the entire army he cast those chosen before the elephants. Every one of them was trampled to death beneath the feet of the monstrous beasts, whilst Philip neither hindered nor sanctioned it and it was evident that he would only endorse happy outcomes.

13.76 This was both a sign and the inception of civil war amongst the Macedonians. Belatedly perceiving the perfidy of Perdiccas, Meleager still stood stiff amidst his formations, since no force was focussed upon his own person. Yet soon afterwards he forsook all hope of salvation, since he saw that his enemies were manipulating the name of the man he had himself made king to procure his destruction *through charges that he plotted against Perdiccas.* Hence he sought asylum in a sanctuary, but not even so sacred a site saved him from being slaughtered.

---

[31] The same Macedonian ceremony is described in more detail by Livy 40.6, but in the context of the reign of Philip V over a century later.

[32] Manuscripts of Curtius 10.9.18 gave CCC (300), but Diodorus 18.4.7 has "thirty", which is preferable: e.g. manuscripts of Curtius 9.8.15 gave DCCC for LXXX (i.e. 10x exaggeration.)

Book 13: July 324BC – July 323BC & Beyond

13.77 Having led the army into the metropolis, **Perdiccas convened a council of the main men, at which they were disposed to divide the direction of their dominions thus:**[33] *that the king should assuredly hold the whole empire in his sway;* **that Ptolemy** the son of Lagus **should be Satrap of Egypt** *and of such Libyan peoples as were subject to the Macedonians;* **that Syria should be ceded to Laomedon** of Mitylenê together with Phoenicia; **Cilicia was for Philotas; Antigonus was assigned to hold Greater Phrygia with** Nearchus to assist him in **Lycia and Pamphylia; they sent Cassander**[34] **to Caria** *and Menander to Lydia; Hellespontine Phrygia was designated as the province allotted to Leonnatus;* **to Eumenes were granted Paphlagonia and Cappadocia** *plus the* associated *coast of the Pontic Sea and he was empowered to protect that region as far as Trapezus*[35] *and to contest its rule with Ariarathes,*[36] *who alone had eluded the dominion of the empire,* since pressing problems elsewhere had diverted Alexander after the fall of Darius; Greater **Media was assigned to Pithon** the Illyrian; **in Europe, Thrace and those nations adjoining the Pontic Sea were given to Lysimachus** and Antipater was appointed to govern Macedon and the neighbouring nations.

13.78 Concerning the leadership of India, Bactria, Sogdiana and those others who inhabit the territories near either the Ocean or the Red Sea, it was decreed that those who had hitherto held command should keep it. In this vein they revalidated the reign of Taxiles and that of Porus as arranged by Alexander himself. Pithon *the son of Agenor* was sent to secure *the satrapy and* the Indian outposts *running alongside their lands.* The satrapy that stretches along the Caucasus range that is called Paropamisus was assigned to Oxyartes *the Bactrian, whose daughter, Roxane, Alexander had wed.* Sibyrtius was recognised as running Arachosia and Kedrosia; Stasanor of Soli in Aria and Drangianê; *Philip for Bactria*[37] *and Sogdiana; Phrataphernes had Hyrcania and Parthia; Peucestes was reappointed to Persia; Tlepolemus retained Carmania;* Atropates, *the father-in-law of Perdiccas,* held *Lesser* Media *and Coenus received Susiana;* Archon *of Pella* controlled Babylon and Arcesilaus managed Mesopotamia. He set Seleucus in command of

---

[33] What follows is the Cleitarchan version of the First Division of the Satrapies, for which the sources are: Curtius 10.10.1-4, Diodorus 18.3 & Justin 13.4.9-23, although Justin becomes muddled for the Eastern Satrapies, which Curtius omits; there are also some significant commonalities with Metz Epitome 116-122; a slightly variant tradition is preserved by Photius.

[34] Probably an error for Asander (cf. Photius: 92 Arrian 156.1.6 & 156.9.37; 82 Dexippus) but common to Curtius, Justin & Diodorus and therefore derived from their common source (Cleitarchus). This suggests that they are all still following Cleitarchus. The same error occurs in the Metz Epitome 117 – did Cleitarchus source his list from the prototype of the Metz Epitome?

[35] I.e. Trebizond (modern Trabzon in NE Turkey); *trapeiunta* or *trapeiuncta* in the MSS of Curtius.

[36] Ariarathes is interpreted from MSS readings: *araba, arbate* and *harbate.*

[37] On the matters of Philip for Bactria and Phrataphernes for Parthia, Diodorus agrees with solely the Metz Epitome.

the Companion Cavalry, *a most exalted status, for first Hephaistion followed by Perdiccas had led them. To construct the catafalque and convey the corpse of the king who had deceased unto Ammon they assigned Arrhidaeus. Finally,* Perdiccas was to remain with his monarch and to command the forces that followed him.

13.79 *It has been believed by some that the satrapies were distributed according to the Will of Alexander, but we have established that this is an unfounded rumour, despite its having been reported by some authorities.*[38] Yet indeed **they had each established themselves in power bases, which after the division of the dominions they defended as their own**, as if demarcation could ever endure in the face of unrestrained ambition.[39] **Thus those who had but recently seemed servants of another sovereign**, safeguarding his suzerainty, **seized sizable realms in their own right;** thereby removing reasons for rivalry, since all were on the same side by nationality and the headquarters of each was isolated from the rest. Yet it was hard to be happy with what opportunity had apportioned, for high hopes make first gleanings seem mean. Hence it appeared to each of them expedient to expand their realms, rather than be satisfied with them as they were.

13.80 It was the seventh day during which the king's corpse had reposed in a receptacle, as the attention of all had been distracted from due death rites by the stabilisation of the state. And nowhere else than in the domain of Mesopotamia does any more searing summer heat set in and to such a degree that crowds of creatures caught in open ground expire, so severe is the scorching of sun and sky, whereby the world is withered as if with fire. Springs of water are both scarce and disguised through the deceit of the denizens, by whom they are accessible to exploitation, whilst unnoticed by newcomers. *Hence hereafter is related what is recorded rather than reckoned reliable:*[40] when finally his Friends found leisure to look after Alexander's lifeless body, those who entered could discern no decay nor even the least livid grey of corruption.[41] Neither was his visage yet bereft of the vitality evoked by the breath of life. Therefore, on being commanded to care for the corpse according to their customs, the Egyptians

---

[38] This is an intriguing sentence, uniquely sourced from Curtius 10.10.5; although some have seen it as a comment originated by Curtius himself, it is odd that he uses the first person plural here, having used the first person singular of himself at 10.8.7; in fact, the related sentiments in the ensuing paragraph were probably not devised by Curtius himself, since Curtius 10.10.6-8 is rather similar to Justin 13.4.24-25 in the same context; possibly "we" means Cleitarchus and Curtius or else is simply a direct translation of Cleitarchus' text; the sentence might equally derive from some kind of *scholium* on the standard text of Cleitarchus; however, the commonalities between the Division of the Satrapies according to Cleitarchus and Metz Epitome 116-118 strongly suggest that Cleitarchus was aware of the "Will of Alexander" as recited by the Metz Epitome.

[39] Every editor proposes some unique variant of the elliptical Latin prototype at Curtius 10.10.6.

[40] This phrase is usually given as a personal comment in the first person singular as if by Curtius himself in modern versions of his text, but the crucial verb *refero* is actually *refert* in the manuscripts, so there is no strong evidence that the comment does not originate with Cleitarchus.

[41] The freshness of Alexander's corpse is related by Curtius 10.10.12-13 and Plutarch, *Alex.* 77.3.

and Chaldeans, as if he still respired, did not at first dare to set their hands upon him. Then, praying that it were proper and pious for mortals to manhandle an immortal, they eviscerated the cadaver, gorged the golden coffin with spices and set the symbol of his status upon his head.

13.81 *Craterus, who was among the leading lords, had earlier led away ten thousand discharged veterans up to Cilicia at Alexander's behest.[42] Concurrently, he carried written commissions that the king had charged him to consummate. But after Alexander's passing his Successors were minded not to proceed with his projects. For when Perdiccas perused plans for the completion of Hephaistion's mausoleum in the memoranda of the king, which demanded much money, and also the rest of his schemes, which were many and magnificent and meant matchless munificence, he decided that it was wise to set them aside. But in order not to detract from Alexander's prestige at the whim of his personal opinion, he asked the Assembly of the common Macedonians to pronounce upon all these projects.*

13.82 *These were the most magnificent and meet of memory among the matters in the memoranda: the construction of a thousand galleys of greater size than triremes in Phoenicia, Syria, Cilicia and Cyprus for the purposes of the campaign against the Carthaginians and such others as dwell beside the shores of Libya and Iberia and the contiguous coastal countries all the way around to Sicily; to hew a highway along the Libyan littoral as far as the Pillars of Heracles; to establish six costly shrines, each at an outlay of fifteen hundred talents; to hatch harbours and develop dockyards at suitable spots as entailed by such enormous expeditions; and lastly to found cosmopolitan cities and expatriate populations out of Asia into Europe and contrariwise out of Europe into Asia, so as to lead the largest landmasses into loving kinship and communality through intermarriage and consanguinity.*

13.83 *The aforementioned shrines were to be erected at Delos, Delphi and Dodona, then in Macedon: a temple of Zeus at Dium; of Tauropolus at Amphipolis; and of Athena at Cyrrhus.[43] Likewise for the latter goddess at Ilium there was planned to be built a shrine that should never have been surpassed by any other. For his father Philip he intended a tomb paralleling the greatest of the pyramids of Egypt, such as some tally among the seven most magnificent masterpieces of mankind. When these memoranda were recited before the Macedonians, despite acknowledging the nobility of Alexander, they nevertheless perceived the projects to be overblown and impracticable, so they determined to put none of those mentioned into effect.*

13.84 Since some writers dispute the circumstances of the death of Alexander, declaring that he died by a deadly drug, it would seem

---

[42] Sections 13.81-83 derive exclusively from Diodorus 18.4.1-6 dealing with Alexander's "Last Plans": direct evidence for their ultimate derivation from Cleitarchus is weak, but all other material in Diodorus 18.1-4 seems to be Cleitarchan, hence it looks as though Diodorus did not switch sources to Hieronymus until 18.5.

[43] Russel M. Geer in the Loeb edition of Diodorus 18 makes Tauropolus a manifestation of Artemis, but the son of Dionysus associated with the Thracian Chersonese would seem possible, given that Amphipolis borders on Thrace; Cyrrhus is Cyrnus in the manuscripts, but it seems preferable to assume that the known Macedonian town is intended.

necessary not to neglect narrating their notions.[44] They say that Antipater, who was Marshal of Europe under Alexander, quarrelled with Olympias, the mother of the king. At first he paid her no heed, since Alexander did not swallow her slanders against him. But, later, as their hatred kept hardening and the king became anxious to mollify his mother in all matters out of filial reverence and when his own great deeds in Greece had reaped his ruler's rivalry rather than respect, **Antipater exhibited sundry signs of estrangement. Then, too, the slaying of Parmenion and Philotas** and the execution of his son-in-law Alexander Lyncestes **sent shudders through Antipater as through all Alexander's Friends.** Finally, there were the cold-eyed killings of the governors of the conquered countries not so many days beforehand. On the basis of these things Antipater supposed he had been summoned from Macedon not to participate in campaigns but to experience punishment. So, to forestall the king's plans, **he assigned his own son, Iollas, who was Alexander's cupbearer, to dose him with the deadly drug.**

13.85 *Certainly, Alexander was often heard to exclaim that Antipater coveted kingship; that he was more powerful than was proper in a viceroy; that he was conceited concerning his renowned victory over the Spartans and made all that was given him his own. They even credited that Craterus and a detachment of the veterans had been sent to slay Antipater. But it is a fact that the potency of the poison produced in Macedon is such that it* consumes crockery and bronze and *even eats through iron, so that solely the hoof of a beast of burden can contain* and convey *the liquor. The spring, whence wells up this vitiating venom, they call the Styx. Thus this was carried by Cassander and brought to his brother Iollas,* that used to wait upon the king, *alongside their other brother, Philip. Antipater had enjoined his son to trust in none save Medius the Thessalian and his own brothers. Hence it was that the partying was resumed in the Thessalian's quarters* **and Iollas,** *who customarily tasted and diluted the king's drinks,* **introduced the poison into** *chill water and, after undertaking the tasting, poured this into* **Alexander's last draught.**

13.86 *These rumours, whatever their credence, were soon suppressed by the power of those whom the tales tainted. For* after Alexander's death Antipater reaped the rule of Macedon and also of Greece, *such that he was in complete control of Europe.* Thereafter his son Cassander succeeded him, so that many commentators lacked the resolution to write about the drug. But Cassander is manifestly revealed by his own deeds to have had an antagonistic attitude towards Alexander's legacies and he successively exterminated the whole house of Alexander.

---

[44] Sections 13.84-86 are based on various matches between Curtius 10.10.14-19, Diodorus 17.117.5-17.118.2 & Pausanias 9.7.2-3; cf. Justin 12.14, Plutarch, *Alex* 77.1-3 & Metz 87 *et seqq*.

Olympias he murdered *through throwing her before the exasperated Macedonians to be stoned*, her body being abandoned unburied. With zestful zeal he raised up Thebes that had been razed to the ground under Alexander. *And he also slew the sons of Alexander, Heracles by Barsine, and Alexander by Roxane, whom he despatched with a drug.* Yet he did not end his own existence exulting. He swelled up with dropsy, from which maggots emerged whilst he still lived. And not long after succeeding as sovereign, Philip, his eldest son, was stricken with a wasting disease, which did away with him. Antipater, the next in line, murdered his mother Thessalonike, the daughter of Philip the son of Amyntas and of Nicasipolis, accusing her of overly favouring Alexander, who was the youngest of Cassander's sons. Bringing in Demetrius the son of Antigonus, with his aid Alexander deposed and disciplined his brother Antipater. However, it transpired that in Demetrius he discovered his murderer rather than an ally.[45] So some god wreaked righteous retribution upon Cassander.

13.87 However, Ptolemy, to whom Egypt had been ceded, conveyed the corpse of the king to Memphis, whence it has been transported these few years afterwards *by our sister-loving sovereign Ptolemy the son of Ptolemy* to Alexandria, where every respect is rendered to the remembrance and the renown of Alexander.

13.88 *These were the events concerning Alexander* in the last year of his reign and its aftermath.

Figure 13.4. Ptolemy (obverse) and his badge of an eagle grasping a thunderbolt (reverse) on a silver tetradrachm coin by the Delta Engraver minted in Alexandria between 305-285BC (author's collection).

---

[45] Cassander died in 297BC and his son Alexander was murdered in 294BC by Demetrius Poliorcetes, who then became King of Macedon.

4. Organisation And Sources

The first column outlines each successive episode in Cleitarchan terms. The second gives the extant sources for each episode. The third cites references to the Cleitarchan nature of the material and the last provides technical comments.

Book 13: July 324BC – June 323BC

Summary	Sources	References	Comment
Destruction of Zopyrion and his army in Europe	Curtius 10.1.43-45		Cf. Justin 12.1.16-17
The extravagance of Harpalus towards his courtesans – his flight to Athens & bribery of the demagogues – his ejection from Athens and his murder by Thibron	Athenaeus 586C-D Diodorus 17.108.4-8 Curtius 10.2.1-3 Plutarch, *Demosthenes* 25-26	Jacoby, Fragment 30 of Cleitarchus	Cleitarchus commonly began (or ended) his books with news from elsewhere. Curtius emerges from a major lacuna in the midst of the Harpalus story. Hammond THA 72 & 157 thinks this is Diyllus, but this is confuted by a close match between the Cleitarchus fragment in Athenaeus and D's version
The Exiles Decree	Diodorus 17.109.1 Curtius 10.2.4-7	C10.2.4,8-12,30=D17.109.1-2 Schwartz	Hammond THA 72-3 thinks D is Diyllus
Paying of troops' debts at 10,000 talents (20,000 in J & A) on planning to send 10,000 veterans home to Macedon	Diodorus 17.109.2 Curtius 10.2.8-11 Justin 12.11.1-3 (Arrian 7.5.3?)	Hammond Sources 285; C10.2.4,8-12,30=D17.109.1-2 Schwartz	Hammond THA 72-3 & 157-8 thinks D & C are both from Diyllus, but I assert that all matches between versions in D & C are overwhelmingly likely to be from Cleitarchus – Hammond is probably wrong to suggest that Arrian used Cleitarchus
The Mutiny (at Opis) - troops taunt Alexander for claiming to be the son of Ammon – drowning of ringleaders of the mutiny in the river – Craterus to lead the veterans home – Antipater to come to Babylon with a force of fresh recruits	Plutarch 71.2-5 Justin 12.11.4-12.10 Diodorus 17.108.3 & 17.109.2-3 Curtius 10.2.12-10.4.3	Hammond Sources 134-6; C10.2.4,8-12,30=D17.109.1-2 Schwartz	There is no evidence that Cleitarchus located the mutiny at Opis – Diodorus implies that it took place at Susa - Curtius enters a further long lacuna during events at Opis - Hammond THA 72-3 & 157-8 thinks D & C are both from Diyllus, but I assert that all matches between versions in D & C are very likely to be from Cleitarchus
Arrival of Persian reinforcements; 20,000 archers and slingers arrive with Peucestes	Diodorus 17.110.1-2		This occurred nearly a year later in 323BC in Arrian - Hammond THA 73 thinks D is Diyllus
Arranges for the upbringing of 10,000 children of his veterans by captive women	Diodorus 17.110.3		Hammond THA 73 thinks D is Diyllus
March from Susa to Ecbatana via Karai, Sambana and the Kelones, where he saw a settlement of Boeotian Greeks	Diodorus 17.110.4-5		Hammond THA 73 thinks D is Diyllus

Organisation And Sources

Summary	Sources	References	Comment
Quarrel of Hephaistion with Eumenes	Plutarch, *Eumenes* 2 Arrian 7.13.1		The only hint that Cleitarchus may have mentioned the quarrel between Hephaistion and Eumenes is that Arrian mentions their reconciliation as a "story", which usually means he did not find it in Ptolemy or Aristobulus (the main source on the quarrel is Plutarch's Life of Eumenes) – there is a similar dearth of evidence for the quarrel between Hephaistion and Craterus in India, so perhaps Cleitarchus avoided this topic
Sightseeing trip to Bagistane - 60,000 horses where once there had been 160,000 - Atropates gives Alexander 100 Amazons	Arrian 7.13.2-3 Diodorus 17.110.5-6	Hammond Sources 293	Strabo 505 Hammond THA 73 thinks D is Diyllus
Arrival at Ecbatana – holds a drama festival - the Death of Hephaistion and Alexander's mourning – orders Perdiccas to conduct the corpse to Babylon for a magnificent funeral	Plutarch 72.1-3 Diodorus 17.110.7-8 Justin 12.12.11-12	Hammond Sources 136-140 & THA 107-8	Hammond THA 73 thinks D is Diyllus, but that J is drawing on Ephippus, perhaps via Cleitarchus and "P's much more sensational account" is Cleitarchus
Unrest in Greece fuelled by dissolution of Satrapal armies of mercenaries on Alexander's orders	Diodorus 17.111.1-3		Hammond THA 73-4 thinks D is Diyllus
Against the Cossaeans	Diodorus 17.111.4-6 Plutarch 72.3		January-February 323BC - Hammond THA 73-4 thinks D is Diyllus
To Babylon – ill omens – warnings from the Chaldean scholars	Plutarch 73.1-4 Diodorus 17.112 Justin 12.13.3-5	Hammond Sources 141-3 Hammond THA 108	March-April 323BC - Hammond THA 74 thinks D is Diyllus
Embassies at Babylon including the embassy of the Romans	Pliny NH 3.57 Diodorus 17.113 (cf. Arrian 7.15.5, Livy 9.18.6) Justin 12.13.1-2	Jacoby, Fragment 31 of Cleitarchus Hammond THA 108	Possibly suggestive that Cleitarchus wrote after campaigns of Pyrrhus made Romans famous in the Greek world, but could simply be true. Livy attacks "frivolous Greeks" who harped on about Romans bowing to Alexander in his digression on Alexander vs. the Romans - Hammond THA 74 thinks D is Diyllus
Hephaistion's pyre at 12,000 talents - anecdotes of Hephaistion's status in Alexander's affections – response from Ammon brought by Philip that Hephaistion should be worshipped as God-Coadjutor (Paredros)	Diodorus 17.114-115 Arrian 7.14.8 Plutarch 72.3 & 75.2, Jacoby Fragment 41	Hammond Sources 139 & 296 Hamilton Plutarch Alex liii	Cf. Lucian, Slander 17, Aelian, VH 7.8 - Hammond THA 74-5 thinks D is Diyllus & Ephippus (however, there are grounds to suspect that Cleitarchus used Ephippus' book on the Death of Alexander & Hephaistion)
Episode of the prisoner who sat on the throne	Diodorus 17.116.2-4, Jacoby Fragment 52	Hammond THA 76-7	Cf. Plutarch 73.3-4

The Death of Alexander the Great by Andrew Chugg

Summary	Sources	References	Comment
Visit to the marshes – Alexander's boat becomes lost for three days – diadem catches on a reed, retrieved by oarsman	Diodorus 17.116.5-7	Hammond THA 76-7	
Drinking party hosted by Medius the Thessalian following a ceremonial banquet in honour of Nearchus - Cup of Heracles – Alexander falls ill	Plutarch 75.3 Justin 12.13.6-10 Diodorus 17.117.1-3	Hammond Sources 151 & THA 77-8 & 108-9 Hamilton Plutarch Alex liii	Cf. Ephippus in Athenaeus 434A-B
Death in Babylon (After 3 days troops filed past, Where to find a worthy king? Body to Ammon, Funeral Games, On 6th day voice failed and gave ring to Perdiccas, "To whom do you leave your kingdom?" - "To the strongest", Divine honours when happy)	Diodorus 17.117.4 Curtius 10.5.1-6 Justin 12.15 Arrian 7.26.3	Hammond Sources 309& THA 77-8 & 108-9	Towards evening 10th June 323BC – Hammond THA 158-9 thinks C did not draw on Arrian's sources, but he is unsure of the identity of C's source
Reaction in Babylon	Curtius 10.5.7-17		
Death of Sisygambis (D: Sisyngambris)	Diodorus 17.118.3 Curtius 10.5.18-25 Justin 13.1.5-6	C10.5.21-25=D17.118.3, J13.1.5-6 Schwartz	Hammond THA 78 & 159 thinks D & C are both from Diyllus, but all matches between versions in D & C are very likely from Cleitarchus
Obituary for Alexander	Curtius 10.5.26-37		
Accession of Philip III: the dispute between the cavalry and the infantry and its resolution in the elephant parade	Curtius 10.6-9 Justin 13.2-13.4.8 Diodorus 18.2 & 18.4.7-8		
First Division of the Satrapies	Curtius 10.10.1-8 Diodorus 18.3 Justin 13.4.9-25		Cf. Metz Epitome 116-122
Preservation of Alexander's corpse	Curtius 10.10.9-13 Plutarch 77.3		
The Last Plans	Diodorus 18.4.1-6	Jane Hornblower, Hieronymus of Cardia, pp.80-97	The lengthy geographical review starting at Diodorus 18.5 probably marks his switch to his next source, Hieronymus of Cardia
Conspiracy of Antipater and his sons, Cassander and Iollas (and Philip) – poison from the Styx brought in a mule's hoof - the rumour was suppressed, because of the subsequent power of Antipater and Cassander; restoration of Thebes and murders of Alexander's family by Cassander; fate of Cassander and his family	Diodorus 17.118.1-2 Justin 12.14 Val Max 1.7 ext2 Curtius 10.10.14-19 Pausanias 9.7.2	C10.10.14,18-19=D17.117.5& D17.118.2 cf. J12.13.10 Schwartz	Cleitarchus may have given this as an alternative as in Diodorus – cf. Ampelius 16.2, which Seel thought a fragment of Trogus: it says it was thought unclear whether Alexander died of drunkenness or poison (cf. Pliny NH 30.16.53) – Hammond THA 78 thinks D's version inspired by Hieronymus and THA 109-111 thinks J's version is from Satyrus and does not identify C's source, but it is more likely (e.g. Heckel LD&T) that Cleitarchus took this rumour from the *Liber de Morte* – NB D & C 10.10.18-19 say this story was suppressed until Cassander died in 297BC

Organisation And Sources

Summary	Sources	References	Comment
Entombment in Memphis and transfer to Alexandria by Philadelphus	Curtius 10.10.20 Pausanias 1.6.2-3	Jane Hornblower, Hieronymus of Cardia, p.93	There is reason to suppose Cleitarchus extended so far as to mention the entombment in Memphis and possibly the relocation to Alexandria (how could he ignore it, if it had just happened when he wrote in Alexandria circa 280BC?) The clues are the fact that Curtius ended his history with this information and the fact that Pausanias mentions the Memphite entombment and the transfer to Alexandria in the context of his having mentioned some Cleitarchan stories (e.g. Ptolemy's birth and Alexander's wound among the Malli/Oxydracae). Pausanias uses Cleitarchan phraseology in speaking of "burial with Macedonian rites" (cf. Curtius 7.9.21). This also implies that most of the information in Curtius on the aftermath of Alexander's demise was taken from Cleitarchus.

8. Bibliography

1) Atkinson, JE, "A Commentary on Quintus Curtius Rufus' Historiae Alexandri Magni, Books 3 & 4", Amsterdam 1980.

2) Atkinson, JE, "A Commentary on Quintus Curtius Rufus' Historiae Alexandri Magni, Books 5 to 7.2", Amsterdam 1994.

3) Atkinson, JE, "Quintus Curtius Rufus' *Historiae Alexandri Magni*", *ANRW* II (H. temporini ed., Aufsteig und Niedergang der römischen Welt, Berlin), 34.4: 3447-83, 1998.

4) Atkinson, John E, "Curzio Rufo: Storie di Alessandro Magno. Volume I (Libri III-V) & Volume II (Libri VI-X)", tr. Virginio Antelami and Maurizio Giangiulio, Milan: Fondazione Lorenzo Valla/Arnoldo Mondadori Editore, 1998 & 2000.

5) Atkinson, JE, "Originality and its Limits in the Alexander Sources of the Early Empire" in *Alexander the Great in Fact and Fiction* (editors: AB Bosworth & EJ Baynham), Oxford 2000, pp. 307-25.

6) Atkinson, JE, & Yardley, JC, "Curtius Rufus: Histories of Alexander the Great, Books 10", Oxford 2009.

7) Badian, E, "The Date of Clitarchus" *Proceedings African Classical Associations* 8 (1965): 5-11.

8) Bardon, H., "Quinte-Curce: Histoires", Paris, Tome I (1947) & Tome II (1948).

9) Baynham, Elizabeth, "Alexander the Great: The Unique History of Quintus Curtius", Ann Arbor, University of Michigan, 1998.

10) Baynham, Elizabeth, "An Introduction to the *Metz Epitome*: its traditions and value", *Antichthon* 29 (1995) 60-77.

11) Berve, H, *Gnomon* 5, 1929.

12) Billows, Richard, "Polybius and Alexander Historiography" in *Alexander the Great in Fact and Fiction*, ed. A.B. Bosworth and E.J. Baynham, Oxford 2000.

13) Borza, EN, 1968, "Cleitarchus & Diodorus' Account of Alexander" *Proceedings African Classical Associations* 11:25-45.

14) Bosworth, AB, "From Arrian to Alexander", Oxford, 1988.

15) Bosworth, AB, "Conquest & Empire: The Reign of Alexander the Great", Cambridge, 1988.

Bibliography

16) Bosworth, AB, "Commentary on Arrian's History of Alexander II" Oxford 1995.

17) Bosworth, AB, "The Historical Setting of Megasthenes' Indica," *Classical Philology* 91, 1996.

18) Bosworth, AB, "In Search of Cleitarchus: Review-Discussion of Luisa Prandi: Fortuna è Realtà dell'Opera di Clitarco" in *Histos* (University of Durham, electronic journal of historiography), Vol. 1, Aug. 1997.

19) Bradford Welles, C, "Diodorus Siculus: Library of History," Vol. 8, Loeb, Harvard, 1963.

20) Brown, TS, 1949, "Onesicritus", Berkeley.

21) Brown, TS, 1950, "Clitarchus" *American Journal Philology* 71: 134-55.

22) Brown, TS, "The Merits and Weaknesses of Megasthenes," *Phoenix* 11, 1957.

23) Brunt, PA, "Arrian: History of Alexander and Indica", Loeb, Harvard, 1976 & 1983.

24) Chugg, AM, "The Journal of Alexander the Great", *Ancient History Bulletin* 19.3-4 (2005) 155-175.

25) Chugg, AM, "The Sarcophagus of Aleander the Great?" *Greece & Rome*, Vol. 49.1, April 2002.

26) Chugg, AM, "The Quest for the Tomb of Alexander the Great", AMC Publications, 2007

27) Chugg, AM, "Alexander the Great in India: A Reconstruction of Cleitarchus", AMC Publications, 2009.

28) Engels, Donald W, "Alexander the Great and the Logistics of the Macedonian Army", University of California, 1978.

29) Errington, RM, "Bias in Ptolemy's History of Alexander", *Classical Quarterly* 19, 1969, 233-242.

30) Errington, RM, "From Babylon to Triparadeisos, 323-320BC," *JHS* 90 (1970) 72-75.

31) Fontana, M, "Il problema delle fonti per il XVII Libro di Diodoro Siculo," *Kokalos* I (1955), 155-190.

32) Goralski, Walter J., "Arrian's Events After Alexander," *Ancient World* 19, 1989.

33) Goukowsky, P, 1969, "Clitarque seul? Remarques sur les sources du livre xvii de Diodore de Sicile", *Revue des Etudes Anciennes* 71: 320-6.

34) Gunderson, Lloyd L, "Quintus Curtius Rufus: On His Historical Methods in the *Historiae Alexandri*" in Philip II, Alexander the Great

and the Macedonian Heritage, eds. WL Adams & E N Borza, Lanham, 1982, pp.177-196.

35) Hamilton, JR, 1961, "Cleitarchus & Aristobulus" *Historia* 10: 448-59.

36) Hamilton, JR, "Plutarch, Alexander: A Commentary", Oxford 1969.

37) Hamilton, JR, 1977, "Cleitarchus and Diodorus 17" in *Greece & the Ancient Mediterranean in History and Prehistory*, ed KH Kinzl, Berlin, 126-46.

38) Hammond, NGL, "Three Historians of Alexander the Great", Cambridge 1983.

39) Hammond, NGL, "The Regnal Years of Philip and Alexander," *Greek, Roman and Byzantine Studies*, Vol. 33, 1992, 355-373.

40) Hammond, NGL, "Sources for Alexander the Great", Cambridge 1993.

41) Heckel, W, "The Last Days & Testament of Alexander the Great", *Historia Einzelschriften*, Heft 56, Stuttgart 1988.

42) Heckel, W, "The Marshals of Alexander's Empire", Routledge, 1992.

43) Heckel, W, "The Earliest Evidence for the Plot to Poison Alexander" in *Alexander's Empire: Formulation to Decay*, California 2007.

44) Heckel, W, "Who's Who in the Age of Alexander the Great", Blackwell 2006.

45) Holt, Frank, "Alexander the Great and the Mystery of the Elephant Medallions", California, 2003.

46) Hornblower, Jane, "Hieronymus of Cardia", OUP, 1981.

47) Howard, CL, Review of the Teubner Edition of the *Metz Epitome*, Classical Philology 58, pp. 129-131.

48) Hunt, JM, "An Emendation in the *Epitoma Metensis*", *Classical Philology* 67, pp. 287-288.

49) Hunt, JM, "More Emendations in the *Epitoma Metensis*", *Classical Philology* 80, pp. 335-337.

50) Jacoby, F, *FGrH* 137, "Kleitarchos".

51) Karageorghis, V, "Cyprus", London, 1969.

52) Koldewey, R, "The Excavations at Babylon", London, 1914.

53) Markle, Minor, "A Shield Monument from Veria and the Chronology of Macedonian Shield Types", *Hesperia* 68.2, 1999.

54) Merkelbach, Reinhold, "Die Quellen des Griechischen Alexanderromans," *Zetema Monographien zur Klassischen Altertumswissenschaft*, Heft 9, Munich 1954.

Bibliography

55) Müller, Konrad & Schönfeld, Herbert, "Q. Curtius Rufus: Geschichte Alexanders des Grossen", Tusculum, Munich, 1954.

56) Oldach, David W. & Richard, Robert E., "A Mysterious Death", *The New England Journal of Medicine*, June 11, 1998, Volume 338, Number 24.

57) Palagia, Olga, "Hephaestion's Pyre and the Royal Hunt of Alexander", pp. 167-206 in *Alexander the Great in Fact and Fiction*, edited by A. B. Bosworth & E. J. Baynham, Oxford, 2000.

58) Pearson, Lionel, 1960, "Cleitarchus" in *The Lost Histories of Alexander the Great*, American Philological Association, London and New York.

59) Prandi, Luisa, "Callistene. Uno storico tra Aristotele e i re macedoni", Milan, 1985.

60) Prandi, Luisa, "Fortuna è Realtà dell'Opera di Clitarco" in *Historia Einzelschriften* 104, Steiner, Stuttgart 1996.

61) Rolfe, John C, "Quintus Curtius: History of Alexander", Loeb, Harvard, 1946.

62) Schachermeyr, F, "Alexander der Grosse: Das Problem seiner Persönlichkeit und seines Wirkens", Vienna, 1973.

63) Schachermeyr, F, "Alexander in Babylon und die Reichsordnung nach seiner Tod", Vienna, 1970.

64) Schwartz, E, Paulys Real-Encyclopädie, Vol. 4, 1901, s.v. Q. Curtius Rufus, cols. 1871-1891, & Vol 5, 1905, s.v. Diodoros, cols. 682-684.

65) Steele, R. B., "Quintus Curtius Rufus", *AJP* 36, 1915.

66) Tarn, WW, "Alexander the Great, Vol II, Sources and Studies", Part One, The So-Called 'Vulgate' and its Sources, pp. 1-133, Cambridge 1948.

67) Thomas, PH, Editor, "Incerti Auctoris Epitoma Rerum Gestarum Alexandri Magni cum Libro de Morte Testamentoque Alexandri" (The *Metz Epitome*), Teubner, Leipzig 1966.

68) Wood, Michael, "Footsteps of Alexander", BBC, 1997.

69) Yardley, JC & Heckel, W, "Quintus Curtius Rufus: The History of Alexander", Penguin Classics, 1984.

70) Yardley, JC & Heckel, W, "Justin: Epitome of the Philippic History of Pompeius Trogus, Vol I, Books 11-12, Alexander the Great", Oxford 1997.

71) Zeller, Eduard, "Die Philosophie der Griechen", 4th ed., Part II, Leipzig, 1889.

Selected Ancient Sources

Aelian, Varia Historia, N.G. Wilson, Loeb, Harvard, 1997

Aelian, On The Characteristics of Animals, trans. A.F. Scholfield in 3 volumes, Loeb, Harvard, 1958

Agatharchides, Agatharchides of Cnidus on the Erythraean Sea, Stanley M. Burstein, Translator and Editor, Hakluyt Society, London, 1989

Arrian, Anabasis Alexandri and Indica, P.A. Brunt, Loeb, Harvard, 1976 and 1983

Arrian, Epitome of the History of Events After Alexander, *Photius* 92, Photius, Bibliothèque, vol. II, René Henry, Paris, 1960

Athenaeus, Deipnosophistae, Charles Burton Gulick, Loeb, Harvard, 1927-41

Curtius, The History of Alexander, John C. Rolfe, Loeb, Harvard, 1946; The History of Alexander, trans. John Yardley, Penguin Classics, 1984; Historiae Alexandri Magni, ed. E. Hedicke, Teubner, 1908; De Rebus Gestis Alexandri Magni, Freinshem et al., Petrus vander Aa, Lugduni Batavorum, 1696; Konrad Müller & Herbert Schönfeld, Geschichte Alexanders des Grossen, Tusculum, Munich, 1954; H. Bardon, Quinte-Curce: Histoires, Paris, Tome I, 1947 & Tome II, 1948

Dexippus, *Photius* 82, Photius, Bibliothèque, vol. I, René Henry, Paris, 1959

Diodorus Siculus, Library of History, vol. VII, Charles L. Sherman, Loeb, Harvard, 1952; vol. VIII, C. Bradford Welles, Loeb, Harvard, 1963; vol. IX, Russel M. Geer, Loeb, Harvard, 1947

Diogenes Laertius, Lives of Eminent Philosophers

Dio Cassius, Roman History, Loeb, translated by Earnest Cary, based on translation by H.B. Foster - reprints of the editions published from 1914-1927

Ephemerides, FrGrHist 2.117

Hegesias, FrGrHist 2.142

Homer, Iliad, trans. A.T. Murray, revised William F. Wyatt, Loeb, Harvard, 1999

Justin, Epitome of the Philippic History of Pompeius Trogus, Books 11-12, J.C. Yardley and W. Heckel, Oxford, 1997; Justin, Cornelius Nepos and Eutropius, Rev. John Selby Watson, London, 1853

Livy, History of Rome, Loeb Classical Library in 14 Volumes

Lucian, Dialogues of the Dead, XIII, vol. 7, M.D. MacLeod, Loeb, Harvard, 1961

Lucian, Essay on How to Write History, vol. 6, K. Kilburn, Loeb, 1959

Lucian, Calumniae non temere credendum, Lucian: Vol. I, A. M. Harmon, Loeb, 1913

Bibliography

Macrobius, Saturnalia, Macrobius: Opera: Band I Saturnalia, Saur Verlag, 1994

Martial, Liber de Spectaculis, De Spectaculis Liber, Shackleton Bailey, Loeb, 1994

Metz Epitome & Liber de Morte, P.H. Thomas, Ed., Incerti Auctoris Epitoma Rerum Gestarum Alexandri Magni cum Libro de Morte Testamentoque Alexandri, Teubner, Leipzig 1966

Nepos, Eumenes in Justin; Cornelius Nepos and Eutropius, Rev. John Selby Watson, London, 1853

Pausanias, Description of Greece, vol. 1, W.H.S. Jones, Loeb, Harvard, 1918

Pliny the Elder, Natural History, H. Rackham, W.H.S. Jones, D.E. Eichholz, Loeb, Harvard, 1938-62

Plutarch, Agesilaus, Lives vol. 5, B. Perrin, Loeb, Harvard, 1917

Plutarch, Alexander & Caesar and Cicero & Demosthenes, Lives vol. 7, B. Perrin, Loeb, Harvard, 1919; Plutarch: The Age of Alexander, trans. Ian Scott-Kilvert, Penguin 1973

Plutarch, Eumenes, Lives vol. 8, B. Perrin, Loeb, Harvard, 1919

Plutarch, Demetrius, Antony & Pyrrhus, Lives vol. 9, B. Perrin, Loeb, Harvard, 1920

Plutarch, Moralia, vols. 3 and 4, Frank Cole Babbitt, Loeb, Harvard, 1931 and 1936

Polyaenus, Stratagems of War, trans. Peter Krentz & Everett L. Wheeler, Ares, Chicago, 1994

Polybius, The Histories, W.R. Paton, Loeb, Harvard, 1922-7

Pseudo-Callisthenes, Alexander Romance, e.g. Guilelmus Kroll, Historia Alexandri Magni, vol, 1, Weidmann, 1926

Stephanus Byzantinus, Augustus Meineke, Stephani Byzantii, Ethnicorum, Berlin, 1849

Strabo, Geography, H.L. Jones, Loeb, Harvard, 1917-32

Suidae Lexicon (a.k.a. The Suda), Ada Adler (ed.), Leipzig, 1928-35

9. Acknowledgements

I would like to express my particular gratitude to the following for their assistance in the research reported in this book:-

The staff of Bristol University Arts and Social Sciences Library

Matthew Wofinden and Centonex for website support

Visitors to the Cleitarchus Reconstruction pages at www.alexanderstomb.com

C. Bradford Welles for recognizing the usefulness of a reconstruction

A. B. Bosworth for endorsing the feasibility of reconstruction

Index

A

Abdalonymus 8, 22
Abu Roash 24
Achilles 21
Adad 23
Adler, Ada 93
Adriatic Sea 61
Aeacidae 67
Aegae 24, 39, 41, 42
Aelian 21, 42, 43, 44, 85, 92
Aetion 21, 22
Aetolians 60
Africa 6, 7, 8, 12, 38, 61, 88
Agathon 34
Agema 14, 15
Agenor 36, 48, 49, 79
Agesilaus 93
Alcomenae 30, 31, 36
Alexander IV 24, 83
Alexander Lyncestes 82
Alexander Romance . 4, 31, 42, 93
Alexander Sarcophagus 22, 23
Alexandria 1, 8, 11, 19, 41, 43, 44, 45, 83, 87
Amazons 59, 85
Amissus 76
Ammon 21, 27, 41, 53, 62, 65, 67, 80, 84, 85, 86
Ammonians 62
Ampelius 86
Amphipolis 31, 38, 81
Amyntas 48, 83
Anabasis 6, 14, 15, 16, 17, 18, 20, 27, 35, 37, 92
Anaxarchus 61
Antigenes 49, 58
Antigonus .. 32, 34, 35, 36, 48, 49, 79, 83

Antipateriv, 28, 34, 35, 36, 40, 48, 49, 51, 58, 74, 79, 82, 84, 86
Antoninus Pius 20
Antonio Tempesta 56
Antonius 12
Arabia 10, 37, 38
Arachosia 79
Arcesilaus 48, 79
Archon 35, 48, 79
Ares 93
argyraspides 31
Aria 79
Ariarathes 79
Aristander 42
Aristobulus 29, 85, 90
Aristonous 30, 31, 72
Aristotle 44
Aristus 11
Armenian Alexander Romance 31, 42
Arrhidaeus 5, 31, 32, 33, 41, 42, 43, 49, 73, 74, 75, 80
Arrian 6, 11, 14, 15, 16, 17, 18, 19, 20, 21, 27, 29, 31, 34, 35, 37, 41, 49, 65, 79, 84, 85, 86, 88, 89, 92
Artemis 19, 38, 81
Arybbas 17
Asander 34, 49, 79
Asclepiades 11
Asia 12, 16, 21, 35, 37, 38, 39, 50, 51, 52, 53, 54, 55, 56, 57, 60, 61, 69, 70, 81
Asians 63, 65
Assembly 25, 30, 37, 52, 53, 55, 71, 75, 78, 81
Atalante 31
Athena 38, 39, 81
Athenaeus 8, 11, 33, 51, 84, 86, 92
Athens ... 11, 21, 22, 51, 52, 60, 84

Athos, Mt 19
Atkinson, JE 6, 88
Atlantic 38
Atropates18, 34, 35, 48, 59, 79, 85
Attalus 17, 31, 42, 75
Attica 42, 51
Augustus 93
Aurisina 24
aurochs 23

B

Babylon 1, 5, 11, 12, 13, 19, 20, 23, 25, 30, 31, 32, 33, 37, 41, 42, 50, 53, 59, 60, 61, 66, 71, 76, 79, 84, 85, 86, 89, 90, 91
Babylonia 35, 58
Babylonian 66, 69
Bactria 39, 79
Bactrian 79
Badian, E 11, 12, 88
Bagistanê 18, 59
Bardon, H 7, 8, 88, 92
Barsine 31, 41, 72, 83
Basilica di San Marco 23, 26
bastard 33
Baynham, E 88
Bel 61
Belephantes 61
Berlin 23, 88, 90, 93
Beroea 34
Berve, H 88
Billows, R 88
Bodyguards 15, 16, 17, 36, 71
Boeotians 58
Borza, EN 88, 90
Bosworth, AB 8, 9, 18, 20, 25, 88, 89, 94
British Museum 43, 44
Brown, TS 89
Bucephalus iii
bulls 23, 65
Burstein, SM 92

C

Caesar 93
Cappadocia 79
Cardia 32, 37, 86, 87, 90
Caria 33, 34, 79
Carmania 79
Carthage 37, 38, 61, 81
Cassander .... iv, 34, 40, 41, 48, 49, 79, 82, 83, 86
catafalque 23, 31, 41, 42, 80
Caucasus 79
Centauromachy 22
Centaurs 22, 65
Chaeronea 22
Chaldaeans 60
Chaldeans 19, 61, 66, 81, 85
Cheirocrates 19
chiliarch 16
Chiliarch 21, 25
Chios 11
Christian 25, 33
Chugg, AM .... ii, 23, 89
Cilicia 37, 49, 79, 81
Clarke, ED 43
Claudius 5, 6, 33, 74
Cleitus 49, 58
Cleomenes 35, 49
Coenus 48, 49, 50, 79
Companion Cavalry 32, 35, 80
Companions 17, 62
comus 66
Corinthians 62
Cossaeans iv, 1, 19, 35, 50, 60, 85
Crannon 30
Craterus 35, 36, 38, 49, 58, 62, 74, 81, 82, 84, 85
Crateuas 36, 49
Cretaceous 24
Crete 31, 52
cupbearer 82
Curtius 1, 2, 3, 5, 6, 7, 8, 9, 10, 12, 13, 18, 20, 22, 29, 31, 32, 34, 35, 36, 38, 39, 44, 46, 50, 55,

Index

57, 74, 78, 79, 80, 82, 84, 86, 87, 88, 89, 91, 92
Cyprus 26, 37, 81, 90
Cyrrhus 38, 81

D

Damascus........................ 42, 43
Darius ... 24, 39, 57, 62, 70, 72, 79
Deinocrates 19
Deipnosophistae 92
Delos................................. 38, 81
Delphi............................... 38, 81
Delphians.............................. 62
Delta Engraver....................... 83
Demetrius 26, 83, 93
Demosthenes 51, 52, 84
Deuriopus 36
Dexippus................. 34, 49, 79, 92
diadem . 12, 19, 22, 65, 66, 71, 72, 77, 86
Dialogues of the Dead .. 41, 42, 92
Dio Cassius......................... 8, 92
Diodorus 1, 2, 3, 5, 6, 8, 9, 10, 11, 14, 16, 17, 18, 19, 20, 23, 25, 27, 31, 32, 34, 35, 36, 37, 38, 39, 40, 42, 44, 46, 52, 58, 65, 78, 79, 81, 82, 84, 85, 86, 88, 89, 90, 92
Diogenes........................... 27, 92
Dium................................. 38, 81
Diyllus 84, 85, 86
Dodona 38, 81
Domitian 8
doryphoroi 14, 17, 18
Drangianê 79
dropsy 83

E

eagle................................ 21, 83
Ecbatana 19, 58, 59, 84, 85
Eclogae 12, 63
Egypt ... 11, 17, 19, 24, 31, 35, 36, 39, 41, 42, 43, 79, 81, 83

Egyptians 80
Eleians 62
Engels, D............................... 89
Eordaea 30, 31
Ephemerides 16, 29, 37, 92
Ephesus 19
Ephippus 85, 86
Epidaurians 62
epilepsy 32
Errington, RM 89
Erythraean Sea 51, 92
Ethiopia 8, 43
Euios 59
Eumenes 18, 29, 31, 32, 34, 48, 49, 59, 79, 85, 93
Euphrates 38, 61, 69, 70, 75
Europe 6, 35, 38, 39, 42, 50, 52, 54, 56, 57, 60, 61, 72, 74, 79, 81, 82, 84
Europus 31
Euxine 34
Events after Alexander .. 31, 33, 41
Exiles Decree 1, 11, 50, 84

F

Falciparum malaria 28, 29, 30
Fate 61, 65, 66, 71, 77
First Division of the Satrapies...iv, 31, 32, 33, 34, 35, 36, 41, 48, 49, 79, 86
Fontana, M 89
Fontana, M 89
Fortune 71
Freiburg Papyrus 25
Freinshem 7, 13, 55, 92
Friends .. 16, 28, 30, 52, 55, 58, 59, 61, 62, 63, 65, 66, 67, 71, 73, 80, 82

G

Gabiene 36
Gaugamela 17
Gauls 62
German 23

97

Getae 50
Giza 39
Glaucias 40
Glaukos 59
Glycera 51, 52
Goralski, WJ 89
Gorgias 58
Goukowsky, P 89
Granicus 39
Greece .. 19, 38, 39, 50, 59, 82, 85, 89, 90, 93
Greek 1, 2, 6, 8, 10, 11, 12, 14, 17, 18, 21, 23, 25, 33, 38, 44, 52, 58, 61, 62, 85, 90
Gunderson, LJ 89

H

Hades 71
Hamilton, J 46, 85, 86, 90
Hammond, NGL 34, 84, 85, 86, 90
Harpalus 1, 11, 50, 51, 84
Heckel, W 86, 90, 91, 92
Hedicke, E 7, 8, 92
Hegesias 10, 92
Heidelberg Epitome 32
Hellenic 58, 62
Hellenistic tombs 23
Hellespont 20, 21
Hellespontine Phrygia 79
Hephaistion .... iii, 1, 8, 12, 13, 17, 18, 19, 20, 21, 22, 23, 25, 27, 31, 32, 37, 39, 50, 59, 60, 62, 63, 64, 65, 70, 80, 81, 85
Hephaistos 21
Heracles .. 3, 31, 38, 39, 41, 53, 54, 57, 61, 66, 70, 72, 81, 83, 86
Herodotus 21, 59
hetairoi 15, 16
Hieronymus 86, 87, 90
Himalayas 7
hipparchs 31
Holcias 30, 36, 49
Holt, F 90

Homer 21, 25, 44, 92
Hornblower, J 86, 87, 90
Howard, CL 90
Hunt, JM 20, 25, 90, 91
hypaspists .. 14, 15, 16, 17, 18, 31, 57
hypomnemata 37
Hyrcania 79

I

Iberia 81
Iliad 21, 92
Ilians 39
Ilium 81
Illyria 36, 54
Illyrians 48, 61, 79
India ... 1, 2, 6, 7, 8, 12, 36, 37, 39, 45, 50, 51, 79, 85, 89
Indica 89, 92
Iollas 28, 82, 86
Ishtar 23
Ishtar Gate 23
Isocrates 11
Issus 24
Italy 11, 62

J

Jacoby, F 11, 12, 46, 47, 51, 62, 63, 66, 84, 85, 90
Justin .. 1, 2, 14, 18, 20, 21, 29, 31, 32, 34, 35, 36, 40, 46, 52, 72, 74, 79, 80, 82, 84, 85, 86, 91, 92, 93

K

Karageorghis, V 26, 90
Karai 18, 58, 84
Kedrosia 79
Kelones 18, 58, 84
Koldewey, R 23, 25, 90
kopis 24
Kroll, G 93

Index

L

Laconia 51, 60
lacuna 13, 18, 55, 57, 84
Lagus 31, 79
Lamian War 59
Laomedon 48, 49, 79
Lapiths 22
Larissa 33, 74
Last Plans ... iv, 25, 36, 37, 40, 81, 86, 87
Latin 1, 2, 5, 6, 10, 13, 80
Leonnatus .. 17, 30, 31, 48, 49, 74, 75, 76, 79
Leosthenes 19, 39, 60
Liber de Morte. 28, 30, 34, 36, 41, 86, 93
Liber de Spectaculis 8, 93
Library 92
Libya 61, 81
Libyans 61, 79, 81
lions 23, 44, 65
Livy 10, 78, 85, 92
Loeb. 7, 13, 19, 38, 81, 89, 91, 92, 93
London 92, 93
Lucian .. 21, 22, 27, 41, 42, 65, 85, 92
Lycia 32, 35, 79
Lydia 79
Lyncestis 30, 31
Lysimachus. 30, 31, 32, 48, 49, 79
Lyson & Kallikles 24

M

Macedon 24, 27, 31, 38, 40, 41, 42, 50, 58, 69, 72, 79, 81, 82, 83, 84
Macedones 25
Macedonian . 1, 12, 14, 15, 18, 23, 24, 25, 26, 30, 31, 38, 39, 40, 41, 42, 52, 55, 57, 58, 59, 60, 61, 65, 69, 72, 73, 76, 77, 78, 79, 81, 83, 87, 89, 90

Macrobius 50, 93
Magnesia 10
Mallian siege 5, 6, 87
Mariette, A 44
Mark Antony 93
Markle, M 24, 90
Martial 8, 93
mausoleum 25, 81
Maximus 12
Media 34, 35, 36, 38, 59, 60, 79
Mediterranean ... 18, 20, 24, 38, 90
Medius 19, 29, 30, 66, 82, 86
Megalopolis 76
Megasthenes 89
Meleager 3, 31, 33, 48, 49, 72, 73, 74, 75, 76, 77, 78
Melissa 12, 66
memoranda 37, 81
Memphis 23, 25, 41, 43, 44, 83, 87
Menander 48, 49, 79
Mentor 59
mercenaries 85
Merkelbach, R 90
Mesopotamia 28, 79, 80
Metropolis ... iv, 12, 13, 53, 60, 61, 76, 79
Metz Epitome 6, 28, 34, 35, 36, 38, 41, 79, 80, 82, 86, 88, 90, 91, 93
Mieza 30
Mitylenê 79
Monophthalmus, Antigonus 36
Moralia 31, 38, 40, 93
Muetzell, Julius 7
mule's hoof 30, 82, 86
Müller, K 91, 92
Myra 23
Myrmidons 21

N

Nakhthorheb 43
Naples Museum 24
Nature 61

99

Nearchus 3, 31, 35, 38, 48, 61, 72, 79, 86
Nebuchadnezzar 25
Nectanebo 43, 44
Nepos 32, 92, 93
Nesaean mares 18, 59
Nicanor 18, 49
Nicasipolis 83
Nicator, Seleucus 36
Nile 24, 43, 61

O

Ocean 71, 79
Odrysians 50
Oldach & Richards 28, 91
Olympia 52, 62
Olympias 32, 40, 42, 51, 63, 71, 82, 83
Olympic Games 52
Onesicritus 7, 8, 39, 89
Opis Mutiny iv, 12, 13, 14, 50, 58, 84
Oracle of Ammon 27
Orestis 30, 31
Orient 71
Oxathres 70
Oxyartes 48, 49, 57, 79
Oxydracae 87

P

paides basilikoi 16
Palagia, Olga 20, 25, 91
Palestine 43
Pamphylia 32, 35, 79
Pantheon 23, 71
Paphlagonia 79
paredros 27, 65, 85
Parmenion 18, 20, 82
Paropamisus 79
Parthenon 22
Parthia 79
Pasas 76
Patrocles 21

Pausanias ... 17, 31, 39, 41, 44, 82, 86, 87, 93
Pearson, L 10, 91
Pella 30, 35, 48, 79
Penguin 5, 6, 8, 10, 91, 92
pentakosiarch 16
Perdiccas 17, 25, 30, 31, 32, 33, 34, 35, 37, 42, 43, 59, 67, 71, 72, 73, 74, 75, 76, 77, 78, 79, 81, 85, 86
Pergamon 23, 72
Pergamon Museum 23
Perilaus 76
Persia 39, 54, 79
Persian .. 14, 43, 55, 57, 58, 60, 84
Persians 14, 18, 22, 39, 54, 57, 58, 61, 63, 69, 72
Persis 12
Peucestes 18, 30, 32, 48, 49, 58, 79
phalanx 15, 73, 75, 77, 78
Philadelphus 8, 44
Philinna 33, 74
Philip ... 17, 24, 31, 32, 33, 34, 39, 40, 41, 48, 49, 54, 65, 71, 73, 74, 77, 78, 79, 81, 82, 83, 85, 86, 89, 90
Philippic History 91, 92
Philotas 9, 18, 48, 49, 79, 82
Phoenicia 37, 79, 81
Phoenicians 61
Photius . 31, 34, 35, 36, 41, 49, 79, 92
Phrataphernes 48, 79
Phrygia 49, 79
Pillars of Heracles 38
Pindar 44
Pisidia 42
Pithon ... 30, 31, 35, 36, 48, 49, 74, 79
Pixodarus 33, 74
Plato 44
Pliny 8, 11, 62, 85, 86, 93

Index

Plutarch 1, 2, 3, 16, 18, 19, 26, 27, 29, 31, 32, 33, 37, 38, 40, 52, 65, 80, 82, 84, 85, 86, 90, 93
Polemon 42
Poliorcetes, Demetrius 26, 83
Polito, E 23, 24
Polyaenus 35, 36, 93
Polybius 9, 38, 88, 93
Polydamas 58
Polyperchon 40, 41, 58
Pompeii 24
Pompey 8
Pontic Sea 79
Pontus 50
Porus 36, 48, 49, 79
Prandi, L 8, 9, 89, 91
Processional Way 23
Proconsul 6, 7
Pseudo-Callisthenes 34, 93
Ptolemy .. 2, 5, 6, 8, 11, 16, 25, 26, 31, 35, 42, 43, 44, 48, 49, 72, 74, 75, 79, 83, 85, 87, 89
pyra 25
pyramids 24, 26, 39, 81
Pyramids 39
Pyrrhus 11, 62, 85, 93
Pythionicê 51, 52

Q

quinquireme 20, 65

R

Red Sea 79
Rhino 7
Rhossus 51
ring 31, 32, 38, 67, 71, 73, 86
Rolfe, J 7, 13, 91, 92
Roman 6, 7, 10, 12, 20, 24, 90
Romans 3, 11, 62, 85
Rome 89
Roxane. 22, 32, 40, 72, 73, 74, 79, 83
Royal Family 33
Royal Pages 16, 75
rudist 24

S

Salamis 26
Sambana 18, 58, 84
Saqqara 25, 43, 44
Sardinia 62
sarissa 23, 24
Satyrus 33, 86
sauroter 24
Schachermeyr, F 91
Schönfeld, H 91, 92
Schwartz, E 46, 84, 86, 91
Scythians 50
Second Division of the Satrapies 34, 35
Seleucus 31, 32, 35, 36, 48, 49, 79
Serapeum 23, 25, 43, 44
Sibians 39
Sibyrtius 48, 49, 79
Sicily 62, 81
Sidon 8, 22, 23
Silver Shields 31
Sirens 25, 65
Sisygambis 70, 86
Sittacenê 18, 58
Sogdiana 39, 79
Soli 79
somatophylakes 14, 15, 16, 17, 18, 30, 31, 32
Sounion, Cape 51
Spain 62
Spartans 82
Stasanor 48, 49, 79
Stasicrates 19, 20
Stathmoi 37
Steele, RB 10, 91
Stephanus Byzantinus .. 93
Stilpo 7
Strabo 7, 12, 19, 36, 39, 44, 53, 85, 93
Styx 30, 82, 86

Successors 81
Suda 93
Suidae Lexicon 31, 93
Susa 12, 31, 35, 58, 72, 84
Susiana 50, 79
Susians 15
Syria 37, 38, 42, 51, 79, 81

T

Taenarum 51, 52, 60
Tarn, WW 6, 37, 38, 91
Tarsus 51
Tauropolus 38, 81
Taxiles 36, 48, 49, 79
Telmissus 42
tetradrachm 13, 83
Teubner 7, 90, 91, 92, 93
Thapsacus 38
Thebes 9, 44, 83, 86
Theopompus 11, 52
Thessalian 66, 82, 86
Thessalonike 27, 83
Thessaly 30, 66, 76
Thibron 52, 84
Thomas, PH 91, 93
Thrace 19, 50, 79, 81
Thracian 38, 62, 81
thunderbolt 83
Tigris 13, 58
Timagenes 2, 6
Tlepolemus 48, 49, 79
Trapezus 34, 79
Trebizond 34, 79
Triparadeisus 36
triremes 20, 37, 81
Trogus ... 2, 6, 9, 10, 72, 86, 91, 92

Troy 21, 39
Tyre 8

U

Uxians 15

V

Valerius Maximus 19
Varia Historia 21, 42, 44, 92
Venice 23, 24, 26
Vitruvius 19
Vogel 5
Vulgate 3, 29, 48, 91

W

Weise, CH 7
Welles, B 16, 19, 89, 92, 94
Will of Alexander 34, 80
Wood, Michael 12, 91

X

Xerxes 58, 72
xyston 24

Y

Yardley, J 5, 8, 88, 91, 92

Z

Zeller, E 91
Zeus 22, 38, 62, 81
ziggurat 20, 63
Zopyrion 50, 84

www.ingramcontent.com/pod-product-compliance
Ingram Content Group UK Ltd.
Pitfield, Milton Keynes, MK11 3LW, UK
UKHW041435180426
11947UKWH00007B/456